We are the UNITED STATES

Publisher's note:

The maps in this book have been designed to tell a story, and show the natural curve of the Earth. They are not drawn to scale; nor do they reflect the longitudinal and latitudinal lines of each state. Please consult an atlas after using this book to plan your road trip!

While every effort has been made to obtain permission for copyright material, there may be some cases where we have been unable to trace a copyright holder. The publisher will be happy to correct any omission in future printings.

WIDE EYED EDITIONS

Explorers, historians, storytellers—say hello to the

UNITED STATES

Get ready to discover this one-of-a-kind country, with more than 50 infographic maps!

You are about to take a trip through the unique story of America. Regional traditions, powerful histories, vibrant communities, hidden secrets: every part of this wonderful country has its own incredible culture to share with the world. This state-by-state guide showcases the story of extraordinary people from all backgrounds who make up the United States. You will meet inspiring activists, superstar sportspeople, influential musicians and writers, innovative scientists, and so many more people who have called the U.S. home. From Louisiana's special blend of African and French culture to Hawaii's Indigenous history, each state is a chapter in the American story. This book tells it in a way you probably haven't heard before, celebrating the many ways to be an American.

Join us on a wonderful tour of the people and cultures that come together to create the United States of America.

EXPLORING THIS BOOK

REGION SPOTLIGHT
These bubbles, featuring a collection of key icons, allow you to discover more about one particular place.

INSPIRING PEOPLE
Meet inspiring people who have a connection with the state.

STATE ICONS
Let your eye wander over the icons that celebrate a state's people, places, and history—history that we continue to make every day!

KEY FACTS
Get to know your state stats with these at-a-glance boxes, which give the low-down on a state's capital, population, and size.

CAPITAL CITY
Phoenix

STATE FLAG
Every state and territory has its own flag. Spot each one waving proudly, then turn to the back of the book to see them all together.

INTRO BOX
With so much to investigate, it's good to have a plan! For each state, you may want to start by reading the short introduction.

Each state and territory map contains information about the people who first lived there, who live there now, and who made it what it is today. Cast your eye over major cities and towns, discover the most signficant events that have shaped the state, and learn all about its contributions to the worlds of food, music, dance, art, sports, science, and so much more. Whether you're looking for fascinating stats, facts about your favorite people, see-it-to-believe-it tourist attractions, or even planning a vacation, this book has everything you need to get to know the people and places of the U.S. At the back of the book you'll find a handy index and a gallery of state and territory flags.

GET TO KNOW THESE SYMBOLS ON EVERY MAP

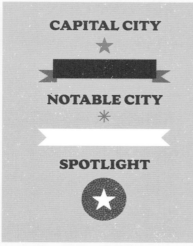

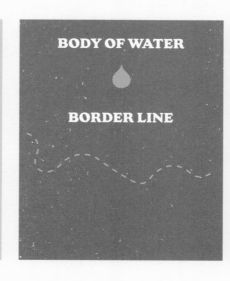

CAPITAL CITY ★

NOTABLE CITY ✳

SPOTLIGHT ★

BODY OF WATER

BORDER LINE

NOTABLE PERSON

REDSTONE WORKERS

The Redstone Arsenal in Huntsville counts astronauts and rocket scientists among its 25,000 employees.

COTTON FARMERS

Known as the "Cotton State," 59 of Alabama's 67 counties are inhabited by cotton farmers.

HUNTSVILLE

CAPITAL CITY
Montgomery

TOTAL POPULATION OF STATE
5,024,279

AREA OF STATE (SQ MI)
52,420

POPULATION OF CAPITAL
200,603

CANE CREEK HIKERS

Residents of Tuscumbia enjoy an amazing 700-acre preserve which includes 15 miles of hiking trails through waterfalls and canyons.

BIRMINGHAM

ROCKETEERS

Huntsville is home to hundreds of scientists and rocket scientists who work for the U.S. Space & Rocket Center.

AUTO WORKERS

Alabama's first vehicle assembly plant was built in 1993. Today, the auto industry employs around 40,000 people in the state.

TUSCALOOSA

TRAILBLAZERS

Hundreds of trailblazers visit Pinhoti Trail, which stretches miles across the state and into Georgia.

SOUTHERN BAPTISTS

The Southern Baptist Convention is the nation's largest Protestant organization, with over one million members in Alabama alone.

MEGAN E. SCHWAMB
B.1984

An astronomer and planetary scientist, Schwamb discovered an asteroid that now bears her name.

MIA HAMM
B.1972

This athletic powerhouse was the forward on the U.S. women's soccer team when they won their first ever Olympic gold medal.

BEAR HUGS

Bear wrestling was so popular in the state that officials made it a federal crime. Today, residents observe state laws that protect bears from harm.

MONTGOMERY

BUMPY TRAIL BIKERS

Dothan's Forever Wild Trails are a popular spot for mountain bikers, who trek through 100 acres of terrain!

MAE C. JEMISON
B.1956

This out-of-this-world astronaut was the first African American woman in outer space.

FRENCH CULTURE

Mobile was one of the first French settlements in the nation and over 6,000 people still speak French or a variation of the language.

CREEK NATION

One of the first Indigenous groups in the area, the Poarch Band of Creek Indians are descendants of the original Creek Nation. This once covered almost all of Alabama and Georgia.

OCTAVIA SPENCER
B.1970

An award-winning actor, Spencer is also an advocate for the neurodivergent community.

CHIEF TUSKALOOSA
D.1540

The leader of a Mississippian chiefdom who are the likely ancestors of the Choctaw and Creek peoples. The famed Alabaman town is named after him.

MOBILE

MARDI GRAS

Mobile was the first area to bring Mardi Gras to the U.S. Today, about one million people celebrate Mardi Gras there.

PEANUT FARMERS

Farmers in Alabama grow half of the peanuts in the United States!

BALLOON-LOVERS

Thousands gather to watch colorful balloons fill the sky at the annual hot air balloon festival held in Foley.

WATER RESIDENTS

Magnolia Springs residents receive mail via river! Locals on the river have enjoyed boat delivery for 100 years due to the land's hazardous muddy terrain.

alabama

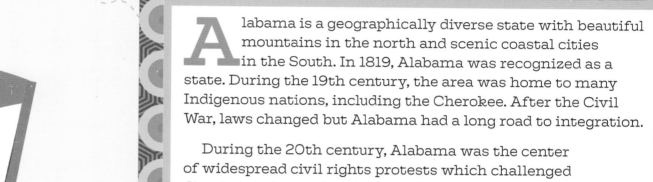

A labama is a geographically diverse state with beautiful mountains in the north and scenic coastal cities in the South. In 1819, Alabama was recognized as a state. During the 19th century, the area was home to many Indigenous nations, including the Cherokee. After the Civil War, laws changed but Alabama had a long road to integration.

During the 20th century, Alabama was the center of widespread civil rights protests which challenged discrimination and racist laws. It would take years before civil rights were granted to every resident. The state also has a place in space exploration history, as the town of Huntsville is the site of a major NASA center. Today, Alabama is known for its strong Southern pride and love of football. You may hear "Roll Tide!" during a regular Saturday drive! That's the motto of the beloved Alabama State football team. Good food, family, and sports are just a few values at the heart of this dynamic state.

KENTUCK FESTIVAL

Residents and art lovers across the South have flocked to Northport for the last 50 years for the annual Kentuck Festival of the Arts. Held during the South's colorful fall season, this festival attracts over 10,000 people. As one of the largest festivals in the state, local residents display art with Southern themes, and musical performers often showcase work reflective of their strong Alabama roots. International artists, such as Toby Foyeh and his band, the Orchestra Africa, have also graced the stages of this popular festival. The festival boasts a unique Southern experience with nearly 300 artists, live music, and folk art. The Kentuck festival is a historic ode to Alabama's art community.

Known for its clear skies and beautiful views of the northern lights, Alaska is the largest state and has a unique and traditional culture made for adventure. This state was populated by different Indigenous groups for thousands of years before Europeans showed up. Alaska is only a few miles from Russia, and in the 18th century, Russian explorers were the first Europeans to settle here. While many settlers called Alaska home, it would take another two centuries before it was admitted to the United States, in 1959. Alaska's small population dominates the nation's fishing, natural gas, and oil industries.

Alaska has the highest Indigenous population of any state, at 15%, and over two dozen Indigenous languages are spoken here. This large state is filled with icy land and stunning ice caves and glaciers. However, climate change has caused some of the glaciers to melt or change in recent years. As the state looks to the future, most Alaskans want to keep their traditions. Many areas are inaccessible by car and people rely on their communities for food, goods, and services, instead of outside help. The pioneering spirit of the Last Frontier remains strong today and showcases the strength of Alaskan residents.

CALLAN CHYTHLOOK-SIFSOF
B.1989
A silver-medal-winning snowboarder, Chythlook-Sifsof is known for winning countless races and standing up for the LGBTQ+ community.

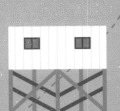

THE PEOPLE OF YESTERDAY ISLAND
Little Diomede is just to the east of the International Date Line, meaning that only a couple of miles west, it's tomorrow! It's been home to Alaska Natives for 5,000 years, who still live here with few modern conveniences.

EVERYONE LOVES FISHING!
One of Alaskans' favorite things is fishing! And one of the most popular places for fishing enthusiasts to visit is Eklutna Tailrace.

OX FARMERS
In Palmer, some farmers have something much bigger than cows to take care of. They harvest wool from musk oxen, huge creatures that used to live alongside saber-toothed tigers!

CHOCOLATE LOVERS' DREAM
Anchorage residents love their hot cocoa! There's a chocolate waterfall in town which, residents boast, pumps more hot cocoa than anywhere in the country!

RAINBOW RESEARCHERS
At the Poker Flat Research Range in Fairbanks, researchers use rocketry to observe the famous northern lights, and even the ozone layer.

CARLOS BOOZER
B.1981
Star athlete and former NBA player for the Chicago Bulls, Boozer was raised in Juneau.

HOWARD ROCK (UYAĠAK)
1911–1976
An Iñupiaq creative, Rock is known for starting the first Alaska Native newspaper, and activism for Indigenous land rights.

RUTHY HEBARD
B.1998
A basketball player for the Chicago Sky of the WNBA, Hebard made *USA Today* Alaska Player of the Year twice!

DANA FABE
B.1951
Known as the first woman appointed to the Alaska Supreme Court, she also was the first female Chief Justice.

Alaska

SUPPLIES FOR OIL WORKERS

Oil field workers stay in isolated areas where cars cannot travel and which may be accessible only by dog sled! Fortunately, the Prudhoe Bay community has a supply store with basic supplies for everyone's needs.

BLUE BABE VISITORS

Researchers and future paleontologists flock to the Museum of the North, Fairbanks, to lay eyes on Blue Babe, a 36,000-year-old mummified steppe bison!

FESTIVAL OF NATIVE ARTS

Since 1973, Alaska Native groups like the Eyak and Aleut, as well as cultures from Canada, unite in Fairbanks for a festival to honor their cultures through art, education, music, and dance.

FLYING AROUND

Many cities across the state are not accessible by car. For that reason, over 7,000 Alaskans have a pilot's license. It may be hard to catch a cab in Alaska, but you're sure to hitch a quick plane ride!

CLIMATE CLASSROOM

The Army Corps Engineers use a Permafrost Tunnel in Fairbanks to teach recruits about different fossils and climate change.

FAIRBANKS ✳ ✳ BADGER

KNIK-FAIRVIEW ✳

★ ANCHORAGE

WINTER WONDERLAND

Yakutat residents are right around the corner from a winter wonderland! The Guyot Glacier Ice Caves welcome explorers with icy walls and beautiful blue hues, which maintain a festive environment all year round.

JUNEAU

GLACIER BEAR LOVE

Alaskans who live near glacier bears—bears with blue-tinted fur—love their furry neighbors! While they may not approach the wild bears, they name sports teams after them and protect them from hunters.

JILKAAT KWAAN HERITAGE

The history of the Tlingit, who have lived in Alaska for more than 10,000 years, is on full display at the Jilkaat Kwaan Heritage Center in Haines. Visitors will learn about how the culture survived in the Alaskan wilderness.

SANTA'S HOUSE

Children all over the world send letters to the North Pole. Well, if you're in Alaska, you can actually see the trading post where Santa receives his letters. Children in the area are on their best behavior—as Santa Claus lives right in town!

UPSIDE-DOWN TREES

A man-made phenomenon, Glacier Gardens is home to a unique forest where trees serve as natural flower pots. With picturesque views, many visitors take photos in front of the area as a beautiful, unique keepsake!

WOLF SONG OF ALASKA

Headquartered near Anchorage, a globally recognized organization called Wolf Song works to protect Alaskan wolves. Founded in 1988, this volunteer organization helps the state's wolves by educating the public through outreach programs, interactive exhibits, and more. The group informs visitors and locals on the plight of the wolf, and works to dissolve some of the negative imagery surrounding the animals. The volunteers even take their show on the road, extending educational programs throughout the state in hopes of keeping wolves safe.

KEY FACTS

CAPITAL CITY
Juneau

TOTAL POPULATION OF STATE
733,391

AREA OF STATE (SQ MI)
665,384

POPULATION OF CAPITAL
32,255

LUCI TAPAHONSO
B.1953
Tapahonso is the first poet laureate of the Navajo Nation.

JORDIN SPARKS
B.1989
An *American Idol* winner, Sparks is a singer and actor.

AI OGAWA
1947–2010
Raised in Tucson, Ogawa was an award-winning poet and educator.

MAX AARON
B.1992
Aaron is a professional athlete who skated to the top, becoming a U.S. national champion figure skater.

HOMETOWN HIKERS
The wide open spaces in this state are perfect for hikers to enjoy traveling the many foothill trails, rocky terrains, canyons, and caves.

HOPI TRIBE
Living in the northeastern area of the state, the Hopi people are known for their artistry, and specialize in pottery, basket-weaving, and the making of traditional kachina dolls.

SNOWBIRDS
A term for retirees who flock to the state for its warm winters. Some snowbirds drive to Arizona in their big RVs, trading the northern cold for warmer deserts.

HAVASU FALLS
For hundreds of years, the Havasupai Tribe has honored a beautiful waterfall on their land. Living near the edge of the Grand Canyon, they also created a unique system of irrigation farming.

YAVAPAI-APACHE NATION
This group lives on nearly 25,000 acres of land and is made up of five communities.

SUNNY SKIERS
Northern Arizona boasts beautiful ski resorts that attract locals who love a quick scenery change. They can sunbathe in one city and ski the snow-covered mountains hours later!

WELLNESS WARRIORS
Sedona is the place to relax! Residents enjoy alternative healing shops and countless spiritual treatments.

DESERT ARTISTS
Scottsdale, Tucson, and Sedona have colonies of working artists. These artists live and work together to create art with a Southwestern flair.

SEDONA

MESTIZO CULTURE
With Indigenous and European roots, Mestizo groups honor their ancestors with special altars filled with gifts or food in what is known as "Día de Los Finados."

ZUNI PUEBLO
An artist community and reservation that educates residents on the unique Zuni cultural art, needlepoint jewelry.

SCOTTSDALE

PHOENIX

MESA

CHANDLER

RIVER DWELLERS
Nestled along the Colorado River and the Mexican border, the Cocopah are known for their skilful river navigation.

TOHONO O'ODHAM NATION
With 28,000 members in a territory the size of Connecticut, this group is the second largest Indigenous nation in Arizona.

WHITE MOUNTAIN APACHE TRIBE
This historic nation once presided over one of the largest Indigenous territories in the U.S. Today, they host hikes, skiing, and fishing for the unique Apache trout on their land.

AK-CHIN COMMUNITY
One of the largest farming communities in the nation, this Indigenous group holds annual celebrations to honor their rich farming culture of cotton and corn.

TUCSON

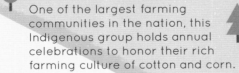

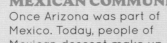

MEXICAN COMMUNITY
Once Arizona was part of Mexico. Today, people of Mexican descent make up 25% of the population.

CHRISTY HAYNES
B.1977
This award-winning chemist is a professor and researcher of biomedicine.

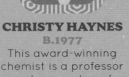

NAVAJO NATION

A historic nation that includes the famous Monument Valley, Canyon de Chelly, and Antelope Canyon as part of its land, the area has a wealth of culture and tradition. The Navajo people were once mostly hunters and gatherers. As settlers began to take over the Southwest, the Navajo had to fight to maintain their land. Today that spreads across 27,000 miles. Many people visit the area's beautiful scenery and picture-perfect views. Locals also provide educational programs to teach others about their vibrant nation and heroes, such as the Navajo code talkers who served in the U.S. Marines during World War II.

KEY FACTS

CAPITAL CITY
Phoenix

TOTAL POPULATION OF STATE
7,151,502

AREA OF STATE (SQ MI)
113,990

POPULATION OF CAPITAL
1,608,139

Known as the "Grand Canyon State," Arizona is a unique place that combines beautiful scenery with strong Indigenous American and Latino culture. It is home to one of the largest populations of Indigenous language speakers. Navajo and Apache are the most spoken of those languages. These groups co-existed for centuries, and encountered European colonizers when the Spanish arrived in the 1600s. When Mexico achieved independence from Spain in 1821, the territory now called Arizona became part of New California. Soon, American colonizers moved there. It officially became a U.S. state in 1912.

Gold, silver, and copper rushes brought in more settlers and a booming mining industry. In later years, Arizona became a retirement community, also known for its thriving Latino communities. The serene views and sacred land are popular among residents and tourists. The rocky state is also a great place for nature-lovers, and has countless retreats. Today, Arizona is one of the fastest-growing states in the nation. People flock to the area for its technology and health jobs as well as for the peaceful living.

ARIZONA

QUI NGUYEN
B.1976
Born in El Dorado, this Vietnamese American playwright is also a screenwriter for television.

DAISY BATES
1914—1999
This civil rights activist and journalist played a huge role in integrating Black students into Little Rock schools.

UFO WATCHERS
Known for its paranormal activity, residents of Eureka Springs host an annual Ozark UFO conference to learn more about the unknown.

CHAPEL OF LOVE
The Thorncrown Chapel is a modern, glass chapel in Eureka Springs, where people go to visit or get married.

SISTER ROSETTA THARPE
1915—1973
This guitarist and gospel-singing sensation is also known as the "Godmother of Rock and Roll."

CHELSEA CLINTON
B.1980
The daughter of former President Bill Clinton, Chelsea is a best-selling author and global health advocate.

SPRINGDALE

FAYETTEVILLE

RAZORBACK FANS
These University of Arkansas football fans have one of the most recognizable calls in sports, known as "The Hog Call."

FORT SMITH

OZARK CULTURE
Covering northern Arkansas, Ozark culture includes stories and songs passed orally between generations.

RICE FARMERS
Each year, Arkansan rice farmers produce over 9 billion pounds of rice! That's the most rice produced by any state.

LITERARY LOVERS
Book buffs make their way to Piggott, where Nobel Prize winner Ernest Hemingway created some of his most beloved works.

JONESBORO

PARKIN ARCHAEOLOGICAL STATE PARK
The Casqui were an Indigenous group in east Arkansas whose early meetings with Spanish explorers are still being uncovered today.

TRAIL OF LIGHTS
During the holiday season, lights and decorations glimmer throughout the town, attracting visitors from across the state.

MONK SAUCE
Those who love hot flavors will love this habanero hot sauce created by a set of Benedictine monks.

HOT SPRINGERS
Once called the "American Spa," Hot Springs city has a natural hot water spring and annual arts celebrations for locals to enjoy.

DIAMOND MINERS
Murfreesboro residents have their very own 37-acre diamond mining area. The only rule here is "finders keepers!"

LITTLE ROCK

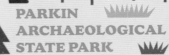

FREEDOM STORIES
Created by Daisy Bates, the Arkansas State Press was the only newspaper in the state dedicated to civil rights and celebrating the achievements of Black Arkansans.

LIVIN' THE BLUES
Residents in Helena honor the legendary sounds of the Delta with their annual Blues Festival.

NE-YO
B.1979
Born Shaffer Smith, this award-winning singer is also a songwriter and record producer of chart-topping songs.

SPOOKY LIGHT SHOW
Tourists flock to a forest in Gurdon to see a mysterious light floating in the trees, and listen to the spooky local legend surrounding it.

WILDLIFE REFUGE
Arkansas is home to wildlife refuge centers that hold abandoned big cats like lions and tigers, who have survived illegal exotic animal trading.

ARKA

THE OZARKS
The Ozarks region extends from northern Arkansas into the state of Missouri. The area is known for its picturesque views and twisting roads, all perfect for those who love the beauty of nature. Once an area where Scottish-Irish immigrants settled, it became a popular destination for tourists in the early 20th century. From lush forests to lavish springs, this region is home to nature enthusiasts of all kind.

Indigenous Americans were the first inhabitants of the area we now call Arkansas. In 1803, Arkansas was part of the territory sold in the Louisiana Purchase. Soon after, European colonizers began to steal the land. The Indigenous population was pushed out of the area, and it became popular for its hunting and fertile land. The Quapaw was a prominent Indigenous group in the area, and soon French explorers began using Indigenous words to describe the land. The Quapaw were known as "Akansa" by other local Indigenous groups, and eventually, this name came to apply to the whole area. It became a state in 1836.

Years later, Arkansas has made great strides to honor the diversity of its state. Today, residents celebrate Indigenous American, African American, and Ozark culture. Arkansas is also a nature lover's dream. Nicknamed the "Natural State," it is a haven for outdoor enthusiasts. Residents enjoy local springs, rolling hills, and beautiful, lush scenery.

KEY FACTS

CAPITAL CITY
Little Rock

TOTAL POPULATION OF STATE
3,011,524

AREA OF STATE (SQ MI)
53,179

POPULATION OF CAPITAL
202,591

TEHRANGELES

More than half a million Iranian descendants—the largest population of Iranians outside of Iran—have nicknamed Los Angeles' Westwood as "Tehrangeles" after Iran's capital city, Tehran. Many community members arrived after fleeing the 1979 Iranian Revolution, but others have been here longer than that. Iranian, or Persian, culture and influence in LA are everywhere, from food and signs to language and style. The Iranian American community celebrates its heritage with the annual Nowruz Festival that marks the Persian New Year on the first day of spring, or Spring Equinox.

BILLIE EILISH
B.2001
Award-winning LA-born singer-songwriter who took the music world by storm with her musical debut in 2015.

CALIFORNIA REPUBLIC

HUEY P. NEWTON
1942–1989
Black revolutionary, best known for co-founding the Black Panther Party (BPP) with Bobby Seale in Oakland.

THE ORIGINAL HIPSTERS
Beat poets came before the hippies. They were part of a literary movement and were referred to as "hipsters."

YURI KOCHIYAMA
1921–2014
Japanese American civil rights activist who fought for and won a formal apology and reparations for the imprisonment of Japanese Americans by the U.S. government during World War II.

THAI TOWN
Los Angeles has the largest Thai population outside of Thailand. It has the world's first Thai Town, which every year celebrates the Thai New Year, by closing off Hollywood Boulevard to set up food, entertainment, and a parade.

INDIGENOUS COMMUNITIES
The state has the largest Indigenous community in the country. The Apache, Choctaw, Muscogee, Hopi, Zuni, Navajo, Blackfeet, Shoshone, Paiute, Pueblo, Cahuilla, Chumash, and Yokuts tribal nations all live here.

WORLD CAPITAL OF MURALS
LA earned this title after Mexican artist David Siqueiros painted the streets in 1932. Today it is a center for street art, murals, and formal galleries.

KEY FACTS

CAPITAL CITY
Sacramento

TOTAL POPULATION OF STATE
39,538,223

AREA OF STATE (SQ MI)
163,695

POPULATION OF CAPITAL
524,943

RYAN COOGLER
B.1986
Oakland native and the director of record-breaking, history-making movie *Black Panther*, about the superhero king of the fictional African country, Wakanda.

BLACK CALIFORNIA
California has the largest Black population in the western United States. One of their many contributions includes revolutionizing hip-hop and R&B music culture. Famous artists include Snoop Dogg, Dr. Dre, Keyshia Cole, and Kendrick Lamar, among many others.

HOLLYWOOD

THERE'S NO BUSINESS LIKE SHOW BUSINESS
Hollywood, a famous district in Los Angeles, was founded by moviemaking pioneers in the early 1900s. It's now one of the biggest film industries in the world!

IFORNIA

ALMOND GROWERS
Spanish settlers brought the almond tree to California, where it has flourished. In Central Valley, Californians grow 80% of the world's almonds.

CHINESE CALIFORNIANS
The largest Cantonese-speaking Chinese community is in California. This is where the fortune cookie was born!

LITTLE MANILA HISTORIC SITE

LITTLE MANILAS
After the U.S. took the Philippines as a colony in 1898, Filipinos immigrated to South Stockton. Historic Filipino neighborhoods, or "Little Manilas," can be found in Los Angeles, Sacramento, San Francisco, and San Diego.

TECH-STARS
Silicon Valley is one of the largest tech hubs in the world! Companies like Apple, Facebook, Google, Netflix, and Tesla call the area home.

LITTLE ARABIA
This Orange County district is home to thousands of Americans from Egypt, Syria, Lebanon, and Palestine. The community, present since before the 1950s, has helped transform the area into a vibrant locale full of restaurants, bakeries, halal markets, and community organizations.

CAMBODIA TOWN
Long Beach, one of the most diverse American cities, has the largest Cambodian population outside of Cambodia. In April they celebrate Cambodian New Year with parades, food, and music.

LITTLE SAIGON
The oldest and largest Vietnamese American community lives in Orange County. Its Vietnamese pop music industry is larger than Vietnam's! The Tết Spring Festival, or Lunar New Year, celebrates their heritage with food, parades, and cultural exhibitions.

People have lived in present-day California for almost 20,000 years. The area's diverse climates and landscapes led early Indigenous populations to split and settle into smaller communities here, and develop their own unique cultures and lifestyles. More than 500 peoples lived in this region, including the Quechan (Yuma), Maidu, Pomo, and Hupa. Then Juan Rodriguez Cabrillo arrived in 1542, claiming the land for the Spanish colonial ruler. In 1848, the U.S. bought most of an independent Mexico's territory in the west, including California. In 1850, California became the 31st state in the Union.

California's climates and environments range from blazing deserts to subarctic regions. It has a few nicknames, including the "Golden State" because of its historical connection with the Gold Rush. It has the largest and most diverse population in the country, and is home to people from all over the world. The state is known for a lot of things, including being a hub for movies, celebrity culture, and inspiring inventions like wetsuits, skateboards, Apple products, Frisbees, and the Internet.

HISPANIC CALIFORNIANS
California is home to the country's biggest Central American and Mexican communities. Southern California is also home to the historic Chicano Movement, which embraced Mexican identity.

HOLY GUACAMOLE!
Fallbrook is known as the avocado capital of the world! At the annual Avocado Festival, events include the "World Championship of Guacamole" and largest avocado competitions.

DOLORES HUERTA
B. 1930
Mexican American labor leader and Chicano civil rights activist who alongside Cesar Chavez fought for the rights of farm workers in California.

RYAN TEDDER
B.1979
Lead vocalist of the award-winning band OneRepublic, which formed in Colorado Springs.

TREY PARKER
B.1969
Actor, animator, writer, and producer born in Conifer. Parker is known for co-creating *South Park* and co-developing *The Book of Mormon*.

CHIN LIN SOU
1836–1894
Called the "Mayor of Chinatown," Chin was one of the first Chinese immigrants to the Mountain West, and is known for his activism and success in Denver.

MELISSA JEANETTE FRANKLIN
B.1995
Five-time Olympic gold medalist in swimming.

CAPITAL CITY
Denver

TOTAL POPULATION OF STATE
5,773,714

AREA OF STATE (SQ MI)
104,094

POPULATION OF CAPITAL
715,522

COIN MAKERS
Did you know the Denver Mint made 15.4 billion coins in 2000? That's more than any other U.S. mint facility! In 2006 the mint celebrated its one-hundredth birthday.

FIVE POINTS
One of the first business districts in Denver to be owned mostly by African Americans. Entrepreneur Madam C. J. Walker lived here and musicians like Duke Ellington, Louis Armstrong, Nat King Cole, and Dinah Washington performed here.

LITTLE SAIGON
Denver is home to a buzzing business district where the Vietnamese American community thrives.

MAKE A RUN FOR IT
The Mile High City in Denver is the perfect place for world-class marathon runners to train. With its high-altitude buildings it's an ideal gym for athletes who want to increase their lung capacity!

ART LOVER'S PARADISE
Bringing art and music to the street, Fort Collins is home to Pianos About Town. This art project sees artists paint pianos, which are then placed throughout the town where local musicians can play them.

FORT COLLINS

BIPOC FARMERS
Black, Indigenous, people of color (BIPOC) and womxn leaders strive to diversify Colorado farming and teach food justice while delivering nutritious, fresh food.

SHOP TILL YOU DROP
The longest continuous commercial street in the U.S. is in Denver. It's every shopper's delight! Its 50 miles of roadway is home to the famous Colfax Marathon.

LAKEWOOD — **AURORA**
DENVER

COLORADO SKIERS
Some of the best ski resorts are in Colorado, drawing skiers from across the globe to the 28 snowy slopes of the state.

BEAN FARMERS
Dove Creek is the self-proclaimed "Pinto Bean Capital of the World," thanks to the many varieties that are grown in the area.

INDIGENOUS PEOPLES
Descendants of the Cheyenne, Lakota, Kiowa, Navajo, and at least 200 tribal nations live in the Denver Metro Area. Today, about 54,000 people in Colorado identify as Indigenous American.

LATINO COLORADANS
Hispanics are one of the largest- and fastest-growing ethnic groups in Colorado. Stemming from the early Chicano Movement, local elections now boast Latino mayors and representatives like Federico Peña, Ken Salazar, and John Salazar.

VOTE ME!

COLORADO SPRINGS

CRIMINAL MINDS
A supermax prison, also known as the "Alcatraz of the Rockies," is located in Florence. It houses some of the world's most dangerous criminals.

MESA VERDE
In Montezuma County you'll find America's premier archaeological wonder. It preserves the heritage of the Ancestral Pueblo community, who lived in these cave dwellings for over 700 years.

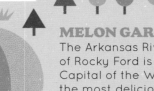

MELON GARDENERS
The Arkansas River Valley town of Rocky Ford is the "Sweet Melon Capital of the World." It boasts the most delicious cantaloupes and watermelons.

RED HOT CHILIES!
Pueblo holds one of the largest chili festivals in the country. Local farmers at the Chile and Frijoles Festival provide samples of the hottest green chilies and delicious pinto beans.

Colorado

The first humans in what is now Colorado settled in the southwest of the region thousands of years ago. Their descendants lived in cliff dwellings in what is now Mesa Verde National Park. Indigenous groups including the Ute, Cheyenne, Arapaho, Apache, and Shoshone tribal nations had moved into the area by the time Spanish explorers arrived in the 1500s. It was the discovery of gold in 1858 that attracted American colonists to the area. In 1876 Colorado became the 38th state.

Colorado's name comes from the Spanish for "colored red," in reference to the red rocks along the Colorado River. The Centennial State—the nickname it was given when it became a state a century after American independence—is home to the Rocky Mountains, the grasslands of the Great Plains, and famous hot springs. Three quarters of its land is over 10,000 feet high! Coloradoans grow some of the best crops, including cantaloupes, Palisade peaches, Pueblo chilies, and Olathe sweet corn. Athletes flock to the area as it provides some of the best landscapes for runners, climbers, and skiers.

MISTANTA
1810–1847
Also known as Owl Woman, Mistanta was the daughter of a Cheyenne tribal leader and is credited with maintaining good relations between the white settlers and the Indigenous peoples of the Colorado plains.

EMMA CRAWFORD COFFIN RACES AND FESTIVAL

One of the most unique traditions in Colorado is in memory of the 19th century local, Emma Crawford, who passed away in Manitou Springs from tuberculosis. Her coffin was carried to the top of Red Mountain and buried there in accordance with her dying wish. However, intense winters and heavy rain uncovered the coffin and it raced down the mountain. Each year, in October, the Emma Crawford Coffin Races and Festival honors her spirit. Participants dress as Emma Crawford and are taken by teams of four in coffin-like vehicles. There's also the unusual Emma's Wake, which showcases Victorian wake and funeral traditions with a buffet feast at the end.

KEY FACTS

CAPITAL CITY
Hartford

TOTAL POPULATION OF STATE
3,605,944

AREA OF STATE (SQ MI)
5,543

POPULATION OF CAPITAL
121,054

JAMAICAN CONNECTICUTERS
West Indians and Jamaicans are two of the state's largest and most vibrant immigrant communities, sharing their cuisine, music, and culture in Hartford events like the West Indian Parade and Taste of the Caribbean & Jerk Festival.

NEWS MAKERS
America's oldest newspaper began in 1764 in Hartford. The husband-and-wife team who ran the paper were rebels supporting independence from England and started a legacy of groundbreaking journalism in the state.

The Connecticut Courant

GLADYS TANTAQUIDGEON
1899–2005
An educator, activist, and Mohegan Medicine Woman whose work in preserving the herbal medicine of coastal tribes led her to found the Tantaquidgeon Indian Museum, the first of its kind in the U.S. to be Indigenous-owned.

MODERN ARTISTS
The Wadsworth Atheneum is the oldest public art museum in the country. It was the first museum to acquire work by Salvador Dali, and the first to host a major exhibition of Pablo Picasso's artworks.

PERUVIAN HERITAGE
The Peruvian community—one of the largest Hispanic communities in the state—celebrates its culture and roots with an annual Fiestas Patrias, a festival providing locals with a taste of home away from home!

TEXTILE WORKERS
For over 100 years, skilled artisans have crafted some of the world's most famous cloth in the state's many mill towns.

MARY KIES
1752–1837
First woman to receive a U.S. patent for a unique method of weaving straw with silk to create beautiful hats.

MARVELOUS MUMS
Florists in Bristol have helped the city earn the name "Mum City," because of how many chrysanthemum flowers they grow and sell. Every year the town celebrates its floral heritages with a festival and parade.

 **HARTFORD**

BUDDING MUSICIANS
Salem is home to the country's first music school, Music Vale Seminary, which was the first of its kind created for women.

ANCIENT TIMEKEEPERS
Horologists are people who study clocks. At the American Clock & Watch Museum they have traced the evolution of time, from sundials and pocket watches to mass-produced alarm clocks.

HAT CAPITAL
Danbury was once the hat capital of the world. It earned its reputation after Zadoc Benedict used a piece of animal fur to plug a hole in his shoe and accidentally discovered how to make felt, which was then used to make hats.

WATERBURY

THE GATHERING
Billed as the most diverse festival in New England, the Gathering is a massive multicultural event held in Waterbury. Every ethnic group in the city celebrates its culture in one place, with booths of music, dance, food, and art.

 **NEW HAVEN**

TREE PLANTERS
The first public tree planting program in America was conducted by New Haven locals. It earned their city the nickname, "The Elm City."

INDUSTRY TITANS
Connecticut has given birth to a handful of successful business tycoons including circus showman P. T. Barnum, TV icon and businesswoman Martha Stewart, and inventor Charles Goodyear.

SUZANNE COLLINS
B.1962
The famed television writer and author of *The Hunger Games* was born in Hartford.

 **BRIDGEPORT**

WRESTLING WARRIORS
ESPN, the world's first sports cable channel, was launched in Bristol in 1979. Today, wrestlers from all over the country head to Stamford House to compete at the headquarters of World Wrestling Entertainment.

 **STAMFORD**

TANGO FESTIVAL

The Connecticut Argentine Tango Academy hosts the annual Tango Festival. Aside from classes and milonga dancing events, the stage production *Tango Passion Show* features the bandoneon and accompanying instruments in a live tango music setting. It even hosts world-famous musicians and dancers. The festival helps showcase the vibrant Argentinian dance and culture as well as building a local love for Argentinian music and art!

HISTORIC BOARDERS

The nation's first boarding school for young African American women was started in Canterbury by Prudence Crandall. Today, it is a National Historic Landmark and a State Archaeological Preserve.

PACHAUG STATE FOREST

The state's largest forest links the tribal heritage of the Narragansett, Pequot, and Mohegan people with the historic Industrial Age mill towns. It is now protected land.

EDWIN LAND
1909–1991
Scientist and inventor, with patents for 535 inventions, including the Polaroid instant camera.

EBENEZER BASSETT
1833–1908
First African American diplomat for the U.S., appointed U.S. Minister Resident to Haiti in 1869.

The first humans in what is now present-day Connecticut lived 10,000 years ago. Over the centuries, the area has been home to peoples including the Nipmuc, Wangunk, and the Pequot-Mohegan. The name Connecticut originates from the word "Quinnehtukqut," which means "beside the long tidal river" in Algonquian, a language group shared by many Indigenous peoples in the area. In 1614, the first Europeans settlers arrived. The Dutch settlers were fur traders. The British followed but by 1776 the colonists were calling for independence. Connecticut became the fifth state in 1788. It earned its nickname the "Constitution State" because it was the birthplace of what is considered America's first written constitution.

Connecticut is the southernmost state of the New England region, and 60% of the land is covered by forests. It is known for trailblazing African Americans who changed the course of anti-slavery movements and for its record-breaking scientists and leaders. It also has a history of ingenuity—the first can opener, phone book, nuclear-powered submarine, and Polaroid camera were all invented here.

HISTORIC CHURCH MEMBERS
Members of the oldest African American church group, the African Union Church, gather annually for a religious festival in Wilmington.

JAZZY SUMMERS
Every summer Wilmington hosts the largest free jazz festival on the east coast, attracting thousands of rhythmic residents and visitors.

WILMINGTON

NEWARK

BEAR

DISC GOLFERS
Hundreds of locals visit the state parks' 18-hole courses as a popular pastime.

MIDDLETOWN

MONSTER RACERS
Nicknamed the "Monster Mile," the Dover Motor Speedway attracts speed lovers from across the state.

DAVID MILLS
b.1938
One of the founding fathers of the Internet, this brainy pioneer developed programming that keeps us connected.

DANIEL NATHANS
1928–1999
This Nobel Prize winning microbiologist discovered new ways to map your cells and received six honorary doctorates over the span of his career.

DOVER

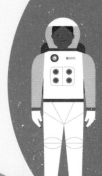

PERFECT BUS RIDERS
Delawareans love to get about on their award-winning rail and bus systems.

SPACE SUIT DESIGNERS
Known for its Space Age designs, one Dover business creates space suits for NASA astronauts.

ICE-SKATING HAVEN
Professional ice-skaters train at the University of Delaware's ice arena—talk about cutting edge!

AMISH UPBRINGING
With a small community in Kent County, nearly 2,000 Amish people have lived in the area since the beginning of the 20th century.

TIGHT-KNIT COMMUNITY
Residents in the Dover area enjoy small communities where everyone knows your name and a friendly smile can be found at every corner.

SPOOKY THRILL RIDERS
This ride isn't for the faint of heart! Considered the spookiest ride in the world, the Funland Haunted Mansion hosts residents who love a good scare.

DUTCH HISTORY
With a nod to its Dutch roots, Delaware hosts an annual tulip festival as well as regional festivals featuring Dutch pottery.

CRABBY LANDING
Residents love crabbin' at Holts Landing State Park, the only pier in the state built for catching these tasty crustaceans.

FESTIVAL HISPANO
With its growing Latino population, nearly 40,000 people attend the annual Hispanic Fest in Georgetown.

PEACHY FARMERS
Peaches aren't just a Southern treat! Peach pie is the state's favorite dessert and local farmers produce about 2 million pounds of peaches every year.

BUSY BANKERS
One of the largest employers in the state, lots of residents earn a living by working in the banking industry.

KEY FACTS

CAPITAL CITY
Dover

TOTAL POPULATION OF STATE
989,948

AREA OF STATE (SQ MI)
2,489

POPULATION OF CAPITAL
39,403

THOMAS GARRETT
1789–1871
This abolitionist was a leader of the Underground Railroad, freeing hundreds of enslaved people before the Civil War.

The second-smallest state, Delaware was one of the first regions to join the Union in 1787. Before the area was settled by European colonists, it was home to the Lenape and Nanticoke Indigenous groups. As Indigenous groups were forced away by the arrival of colonists, the Dutch became the first group of European settlers. Delaware continued to grow, but the small state took its time in attracting more people. It remains the only state with just three counties!

You'll find distinct differences in each part of the state. Residents can enjoy the laid-back vibe of northern Delaware or the bustling busyness of cities like Wilmington. Immigrants from Puerto Rico and South America have added even more culture to the state, boosting the once tiny population. No matter where you land, the clean, beautiful beach views and lush scenery add to the Diamond State's strong appeal.

JOE BIDEN
B.1942
The 46th President of the United States, Biden was a popular senator in Delaware before becoming the leader of the free world.

NANCY CURRIE
B.1958
An award-winning NASA scientist and colonel, Currie participated in four space shuttle missions, spending 1,000 hours in space.

FENWICK ISLANDERS

With a population of a little over 300 people, Fenwick Island is Delaware's best kept secret! Popularly named, alongside Bethany Beach, as one of the "Quiet Resorts" of Delaware, this island boasts beautiful coastal scenery, walking trails, and peaceful living. But most interesting about this tiny island is the people. A tight-knit community, Fenwick is home to a lot of older or retired adults. They are attracted by Fenwick's landscape and its small-town feel. Many residents work for science and technology employers on and off the island. Living by the sea may be a breeze, but if you are lucky enough to call this island home, you are also never far from bustling coffee shops and restaurants.

With over 21 million residents, Florida is a melting pot of cultures and the third most populous state. Before it was home to so many diverse cultures, the region was occupied by Indigenous Americans. They lived here almost 14,000 years before the first European colonizer, Juan Ponce de León, arrived. Then Florida was ruled by both Spain and Great Britain before it was admitted to the Union as the 27th state in 1845. But the partnership was uneasy. A few years later, Florida seceded from the Union as one of the seven Confederate states. After the Civil War, railroads played a major role in the state's growth. Soon, Florida's economy expanded with agricultural products like citrus fruits, sugarcane, and cattle. These changes attracted immigrants from countries like Haiti and Cuba, who saw an opportunity for a better life.

Today, the Sunshine State includes a diverse population of Cuban, Hispanic, Jewish, and Haitian Americans. The warm region also attracts a large retirement population and visitors who love the popular beaches and theme parks. The diversity boom, as well as the weather and unique landscape, has made Florida the vibrant and welcoming state it is today.

TALLAHASSEE

GATOR NEIGHBORS
Over one million alligators call Florida home. Residents can often find the ancient reptiles sunbathing on golf courses or crossing busy streets!

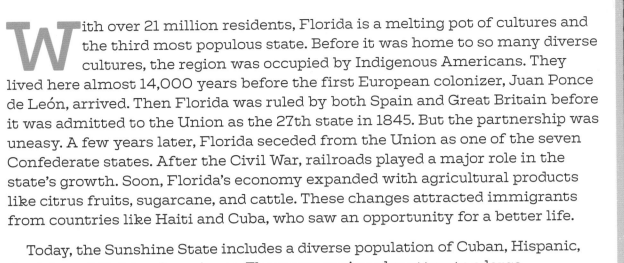

MAYA RUDOLPH
B.1972
Actor and comedian best known for her political satire and impersonations.

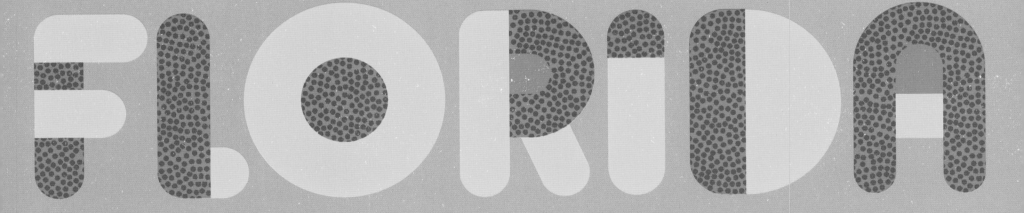

FLORIDA

HAITIAN CREOLE
Residents of Little Haiti enjoy arts, dance, food, and language that feel just like those of the country of Haiti. After English and Spanish, Haitian Creole is the third most commonly spoken language in Florida. Little Haiti, an area filled with Haitian residents, culture, and history, is one place where you can hear Haitian Creole being used every day. The language is a mixture of West African dialect and French. Today, it is spoken by 300,000 Florida locals.

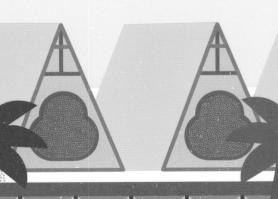

MOUSE-KATEERS

There's no fan like a Disney fan! Thousands of people visit the Disney World theme park in Orlando at least once a year, but locals get to visit as often as they like.

JACKSONVILLE

ALEX RODRIGUEZ
B.1975

Award-winning baseball player who hits a home run both on the field and off, as he has given nearly $4 million to charity!

ARIANA GRANDE
B.1993

Best-selling singer and actor known for her wide vocal range and ability to reach the highest register, or notes, of the human voice.

CAPITAL CITY
Tallahassee

TOTAL POPULATION OF STATE
21,538,187

AREA OF STATE (SQ MI)
65,758

POPULATION OF CAPITAL
196,169

SEMINOLE TRIBE

One of the earliest Indigenous groups to settle in what we now call Florida. There are six reservations across the state and over 2,000 members.

ORLANDO

THE HIGHWAYMEN

This group of African American painters exhibits art showcasing Florida's tropical landscape on scraps of salvaged material.

COOL CARIBBEANS

Fort Lauderdale is home to one of the highest population of Jamaican Americans. Locals fill up on delicious rice and peas or oxtails. Yum!

TAMPA

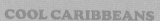

MERENGUE MOVERS

Immigrants from the Dominican Republic have brought new moves and sounds to sunny Florida. Couples twist and turn to the beat when they dance the merengue.

JAMES ROBERT CADE
1927–2007

Sports lover who invented the popular sports drink Gatorade, after researching how athletes lose water and nutrients during games.

ST PETERSBURG

COLLARD GREEN CUISINE

Tampa residents enjoy bowls of flavor at the annual Collard Green Festival.

GOLFER'S HAVEN

With 167,000 players and 1,400 golf courses, golfers can be found all over Florida. Famous golfers like Tiger Woods call Florida home.

ELLEN OCHOA
B.1958

An engineer and former astronaut, Ochoa is the first Hispanic woman to go to space and the first Hispanic Director of the Johnson Space Center.

HIALEAH HOMES

With street signs in Spanish, the Hialeah neighborhood is home to many Cuban Americans. Nearly 70% of all Cuban people in the United States live in Florida.

GUAGUAS ESCOLARES
7AM-7PM

MIAMI

MICCOSUKEE TRIBE

Today's 600 Miccosukee members are direct descendants of a small group who escaped capture by Europeans by hiding in the Everglades.

FOLKLIFE FRIENDS

Every Friday, locals head down to the historically Black Overtown district to explore the history and sample international food, arts, and live music.

THE DOMINO EFFECT

Locals who love a good game of dominoes can walk to Domino Park to play and watch skilled opponents at any time of day.

COLOMBIAN DANCERS

Locals enjoy grooving to the congo and fandango beats of the folk dance group Puerto de Oro de Colombia, whose musicians and dancers showcase traditional dance moves from Colombia.

CALLE OCHO

The Calle Ocho Festival is the biggest Hispanic festival in the state and held in the Little Havana district.

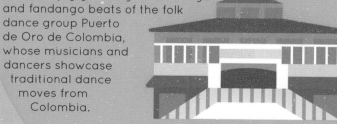

BAHAMIAN GROOVES

Residents of the Coconut Grove area of Miami enjoy a bayfront village with a rich Bahamian culture of easygoing fun and delicious food inspired by African, American, and British influences.

BIGFOOT HUNTERS
Monster and legend enthusiasts gather in Cherry Log, which is home to a large collection of folklore and artifacts of the legendary big creature.

PEACHY RUNNERS
Each year over 60,000 runners meet in Atlanta for the Peachtree Road Race. It's one of the largest 10K footraces in the world.

FRIENDLY FLYERS
Over 110 million passengers per year fly through the Hartsfield-Jackson Atlanta International Airport. Known as the world's busiest airport, it employs nearly 55,300 people.

GOAT HOARDERS
Folks can travel to Tiger to become certified goat rangers! Here goat lovers can meet and feed goats on the roof of a quirky souvenir shop and petting zoo.

LAOTIAN FAITH
Nearly 4,000 Laotians live in the Atlanta area, worshipping at one of four Laotian Buddhist temples there.

TOTALLY TIMBER
Georgia boasts some of the highest production of timber in the U.S. Over 54,000 foresters work on nearly 24 million acres of tree farms.

AUGUSTA

ERIC NAM
B.1988
Singer and songwriter of Korean descent who was raised in Atlanta. Nam is also a television host.

STACEY ABRAMS
B.1973
An accomplished politician and voting rights activist, Abrams was the first African American woman to deliver a response to the State of the Union Address in 2019.

JON OSSOFF
B.1987
In 2021, Ossoff became the youngest member of the Senate and only the second Jewish senator from the South.

ATLANTA

THE VARSITY

DRIVE-IN DINERS
Over 30,000 people per day visit the Varsity drive-in restaurant during Georgia Tech Yellow Jackets' home football games.

HIP-HOP HISTORIANS
A major hip-hop culture hub, Atlanta is a city known for its beat! It is one of the best places to find new music, artists and styles.

FANTASTIC FILMMAKERS
Georgia is the number one filming location in the South! Popular movies *The Hunger Games* and *Spider-Man* have been filmed in the Atlanta area.

MACON

SAVANNAH

HINDU BELIEVERS
With beautiful temples and celebrations, Hinduism is one of the fastest-growing religions in Georgia. Over 40,000 Hindu people worship near the Atlanta area.

SPOOKY STORIES
Many of America's best Southern Gothic writers, like Flannery O'Connor and Erskine Caldwell, used Georgia as the setting of their dark novels.

COLUMBUS

MOREHOUSE MEN
Based in Atlanta, Morehouse is the only historically Black all-male college. Morehouse men, or alumni, hold high standards in academic and professional success.

RAINBOW WALKERS
Atlanta residents and visitors can walk through the Atlanta Rainbow Crosswalks, a colorful LGBTQ+ memorial meant as a symbol of unity and acceptance.

PEANUT FARMERS
Georgia is the number-one peanut-producing state thanks to local peanut farmers, who yield a whopping 2.4 billion pounds of peanuts a year!

NEWSY NEIGHBORS
Thousands of Georgians work at the CNN Center in Atlanta, the largest news studio in the state.

ALVIN KAMARA
B.1995
An American football player, who is the second player in NFL history to score six rushing touchdowns in one game.

KEISHA LANCE BOTTOMS
B.1970
A politician who was elected mayor of Atlanta in 2017. She became just the second African American woman to serve as mayor.

Georgia

KEY FACTS

CAPITAL CITY
Atlanta

TOTAL POPULATION OF STATE
10,711,908

AREA OF STATE (SQ MI)
59,425

POPULATION OF CAPITAL
498,715

Known as the "Peach State," Georgia's culture is filled with Southern pride and charm. With rolling hills and lush forests, Georgia was one of the first Southern territories to become a state in 1788. The growth of the area was heavily dependent on enslaved labor to run its large tobacco and cotton plantations. Following the American Civil War, slavery was outlawed and many cities had to be rebuilt. However, racial tensions remained. But Georgians are resilient and eventually many, including an Atlanta-born minister, Dr. Martin Luther King, Jr., led the historic civil rights movement.

Today, the people of Georgia are the number-one producers of peanuts. And their lush forests contribute to being one of the top states for timber. But there's much more to boast about in Georgia. Atlanta is one of the most diverse cities in America. Hip-hop musicians from all over the world flock to the capital in the hopes of becoming the next star. As the state becomes more diverse, Georgia residents promise to maintain their strong sense of community and historic Southern hospitality.

SPELMAN WOMEN

A historic Black liberal arts college, Spelman is the only African American all-female school in the nation. The college was founded in 1881 by two women, to educate Black women who were not allowed to enroll in white colleges. Soon, enrollment grew and the school expanded. It became known for its strong academics and professional alumnae, or female graduates. Today, Spelman has the highest graduation rate among HBCUs (historically Black colleges and universities). It also boasts several distinguished alumnae such as children's activist Marian Wright Edelman and Pulitzer Prize-winning novelist Alice Walker.

23

With 137 volcanic islands, Hawaii is the only island and tropical state. Thousands of years ago, Polynesian islanders canoed across the Pacific Ocean to reach Hawaii, and became its first inhabitants. For centuries, they lived here until European settlers arrived in the 1700s. The islands were a useful harbor and source of supplies, but Europeans also brought diseases against which the isolated nations had no immunity. The indigenous population decreased, and in 1898, the U.S. forced the Hawaiian Queen Lili'uokalani to give up her rule and Hawaii became a U.S. territory. In 1959 it was recognized as America's 50th state.

It has continued to attract people from everywhere, making it one of the most diverse areas in the country. It is the only state with an Asian American majority, with a rainbow of cultures and people from China, Japan, the Philippines, and Korea. Known as the "Aloha State," its gifts to the world include surfing, hula, lu'aus, and more.

PINEAPPLE FARMERS
The Dole Plantation maze also doubles up as a pineapple farm, with more than 14,000 plants! It was pineapple farming that inspired thousands of Asians to move to Hawaii.

HAWAIIAN ROYALTY
An ancient henge, the Kukaniloko Birthstones lie at the center of Oahu. Many members of Hawaii's royal family were born at this important site.

KAUA'I

NI'HAU

BARACK OBAMA
B. 1961
44th President of the United States. Obama was the first African American president and the only American president ever to be born in Hawaii.

ISABELLA AIONA ABBOTT
1919–2010
The first Indigenous Hawaiian woman to receive a PhD in science. She was a leading expert on Pacific marine algae.

ELLISON ONIZUKA
1946–1986
Hawaiian-born NASA astronaut who became the first Asian American and first person of Japanese ancestry to fly into space in 1985.

THE PRINCE LOT HULA FESTIVAL
The Prince Lot Hula Festival is the largest hula event in Hawaii. This annual event celebrates the Prince-turned-King, Lot Kapuāiwa, who reinstated the once banned spiritual dance. Hula is a Polynesian dance used to tell stories visually. Every movement represents the words of the spiritual Oli (chant) or Mele (song) that accompanies it. The festival showcases island culture with Hawaiian art, music, and food.

HAWAII

STRUMMING STRINGS OF STEEL
In 1885, Hawaiian Joseph Kekuku invented the steel guitar, which has influenced many genres of American music, including country and blues.

JASON MOMOA
B.1979
The famous *Aquaman* actor, born in Honolulu, took a leading role in protesting the construction of the Thirty Meter Telescope on the sacred volcano Mauna Kea.

- O'AHU
- PEARL CITY
- HONOLULU
- MOLOKA'I

HAWAIIAN LIONS
A small team cares for over 500 feral cats at the Lanai Cat Sanctuary. These "Hawaiian Lions" are descended from the first cats brought to Hawaii, by whaling boats over a century ago.

- LANA'I
- MAUI
- KAHO'OLAWE

ANIMAL FRIENDS
Conservationists at the world's largest dormant volcano, Maui's Mount Haleakala, work to protect its unique flora and fauna, including the rare state bird, the nene.

MUSLIM ARTISTS
Honolulu's Shangri La Museum is a collection of Islamic art with over 3,500 artifacts. Every year, two Muslim artists are invited to exhibit their artwork here.

MARINE BIOLOGISTS
Moku o Lo'e or Coconut Island is the site of the Institute of Marine Biology, where scientists study ocean life.

JAPANESE BUDDHISTS
Oahu's Byodo-In Temple is a replica of a famous Buddhist temple in Kyoto, Japan. It is dedicated to Japanese Americans, one of the largest ethnic groups in Hawaii.

UNIQUE UKULELEISTS
The ukulele is often considered Hawaii's national instrument. Oahu's annual Ukulele Festival is the world's largest celebration of its kind. One hundred ukuleles are given away to visitors!

SPECTACULAR SURFERS
In Waikiki, surfers can find some of the best waves, or pay a visit to the statue of surf icon Duke Kahanamoku.

KEY FACTS

CAPITAL CITY
Honolulu

TOTAL POPULATION OF STATE
1,455,271

AREA OF STATE (SQ MI)
10,932

POPULATION OF CAPITAL
350,964

BRUNO MARS
B.1985
Born in Waikiki, music artist Bruno Mars first performed in his family's band, where he became known for his Elvis impersonation.

COFFEE CONNOISSEURS
Kona Coffee Living History Farm commemorates the Uchida family, Japanese immigrants who utilized Hawaii's nutrient-rich volcanic soil to grow world-class coffee.

GREAT ATHLETES
The iconic Ironman triathlon began in Hawaii. Every year world-class athletes compete for 17 hours to finish an epic series of races.

- HAWAI'I
- HILO

HAWAII'S KAMA'AINA
Meaning "child of that which feeds me," this term refers to natives of Hawaii as well as their environmentally friendly lifestyles.

NIGHTMARCHERS
In Hawaiian legend, these ghosts of ancient warriors rise from burial sites or the ocean to honor Hawaiian gods.

LAVA EXPLORERS
The Lava Tree State Monument is a forest of tree trunks that were preserved in lava, after an eruption in 1790. The lava-shaped trees conserve the natural history of the volcanic islands.

PHILO T. FARNSWORTH
1906–1971
Born in Risby, Farnsworth invented the first all-electronic television at just 24 years old.

EMMA EDWARDS GREEN
1856–1942
Green was born in California, and is the only woman to have designed a state seal: Idaho's!

THOMAS "LES" PURCE
B.1946
The grandson of pioneering Black Idahoans, Purce became Idaho's first Black mayor in 1976.

FANTASTIC FIDDLERS
Weiser is known as the "Fiddling Capital of the World." Every year, it holds the battle-of-the-bands-inspired National Oldtime Fiddlers' Contest.

GREEN THUMBS
Idahoans hold lavender festivals throughout the year and across the state in celebration of the herb that is grown on many farms here.

SHOSHONE-PAIUTE TRIBES
Celebration Park displays petroglyphs carved into rocks by the Shoshone-Paiute people nearly 10,000 years ago. Their descendants still live in the neighboring Duck Valley Indian Reservation.

MORMONS
Mormons are the biggest religious group in Idaho and one of the oldest voting blocs in its state history.

YOGURT MAKERS
Many refugees from Iraq, Afghanistan, and Sub-Saharan Africa work at the world's largest yogurt facility, Chobani, in Twin Falls. Chobani was founded by the Tent Partnership to provide refugees with work.

COEUR D'ALENE

EXCAVATORS
Cooper's Ferry is one of America's oldest archaeology sites. There is evidence here that the first people to arrive in North America might have paddled across the Pacific.

DOG LOVERS
Dog Bark Park Inn, a bed and breakfast in Cottonwood, is shaped like a giant beagle—the biggest in the world. Statistically, dog ownership is the highest in Idaho!

SPOOKY SHOPPING
The Sluice Box is an antiques store overflowing with vintage trinkets. This strange, multi-story building is rumored to be haunted by Idaho's pioneering families.

UNIQUE! The Entrepot in Idaho City — Everyone Stops

MERIDIAN

BOISE

PICABO STREET
B.1971
Born in Triumph, Street was one of the greatest downhill skiers in American history, winning a gold medal at the 1998 Winter Olympics.

CHIEF JOSEPH
1840–1904
Nez Perce leader known for one of the most masterful fighting retreats in military history. With only 200 warriors, he fought the U.S. Army 14 times and managed to take his people 1,170 miles before finally surrendering.

FREAK ALLEY ARTISTS
Graffiti artists showcase their work at Freak Alley in Boise, the largest outdoor art gallery in the Northwest.

THE BASQUE PEOPLE
The largest U.S. population of Basque people live in Boise. Originating from Spain, their language is one of the oldest in the world!

ROCK STARS
The Black Cliffs along the Boise River in Treasure Valley are a towering range of lava rocks ideal for climbing.

BLACK HISTORY
Boise's Black History Museum was constructed in 1921 in Idaho's first African American church. It celebrates Idaho's Black history, including the life of York, the only African American on the Lewis and Clark expedition.

DANCING ON ICE
The world-famous Sun Valley Ice Show showcases ice-skating stars, including world champions and Olympians.

IDAHO FALLS

TWIN FALLS

ROCK HOUNDS
Craters of the Moon is a national monument with three major lava fields, 15,000-year-old volcanic cones, and the deepest rift on Earth. It's a prime spot for fossil finding, or "rockhounding!"

POTATO FARMERS
Idaho harvests about 13 billion pounds of potatoes every year. One-third of all American potatoes are grown by Idahoans!

IDAHO

KEY FACTS

CAPITAL CITY
Boise

TOTAL POPULATION OF STATE
1,839,106

AREA OF STATE (SQ MI)
83,569

POPULATION OF CAPITAL
235,684

Archaeologists recently discovered a tool made of rock in Idaho. This was a huge discovery! It was more than 16,600 years old and is now the earliest evidence of humans in North America. Thousands of years after the tool-maker lived, Indigenous groups including the Shoshone and the Nez Perce inhabited the land. It's one of the last places in North America that Europeans took over and did not become a state until 1890.

Today, with its snow-capped mountains, vast lakes, and steep canyons, Idaho has the largest area of protected wilderness in the country. It's called the "Gem State" for the 72 types of precious and semi-precious stones mined within its borders, including the rare star garnet. It's famous for its natural beauty, abundant trout, and being the nation's largest producer of the world's most versatile vegetable: the potato!

LUMBERJACK DAYS

Northern Idaho has long been known as timber territory. In tribute to its logging history, Orofino holds Lumberjack Days, an annual festival which includes a log-sawing obstacle course, log rolling races, and a parade involving "Lumberjack Royalty"—teen ambassadors crowned to promote the lumberjack legacy as well as the festival itself.

KEY FACTS

CAPITAL CITY
Springfield

TOTAL POPULATION OF STATE
12,812,508

AREA OF STATE (SQ MI)
57,914

POPULATION OF CAPITAL
114,394

FRED HAMPTON
1948–1969
Civil rights leader and founding member of Illinois' Black Panther Party, who fought against racism and police brutality.

CHICAGO MUSLIMS
Illinois has the largest Muslim population in the country. The Chicago Muslim Green Team runs eco-friendly projects to restore the balance between people and nature.

BAHÁ'Í
In Wilmette, worshippers of Bahá'í, a faith celebrating all religions, come together in the largest and oldest Bahá'í House of Worship.

LITTLE INDIA
Devon Avenue is known as "Little India" but it's home to Pakistanis, Nepalis, Bangladeshis, and other South Asians. The street is a colorful mix of eateries and shops where several different languages are spoken.

THE FERMILAB
The Fermi National Accelerator Laboratory has some of the most advanced physics tech in the world. Scientists here explore questions about space, time, and the universe.

SUPERCOMPUTER SCIENTISTS
The Blue Waters Supercomputer can perform more than 13 quadrillion calculations in a second! Scientists use it to solve all types of problems, from improving satellites to understanding evolution.

PUMPKIN FARMERS
Morton is the pumpkin capital of the world! Over 85% of the world's canned pumpkin is produced here.

UNUSUAL WORLD RECORD HOLDERS
Casey's town motto is "Big Things, Small Town." It is home to the world's largest mailbox, wind chime, and golf tee, among other giant objects!

CAHOKIA MOUNDS
Over 1,300 years ago, the Cahokia people built the largest Indigenous American settlement north of Mexico, using nearly 50 million cubic feet of earth.

Millions of years ago Illinois was underwater. Over centuries, land shifted and glaciers melted, leaving the region with a mix of hills, plains, and rivers—even one that flows backward! The earliest people in Illinois lived here nearly 12,000 years ago. Their descendants made Cahokia a bustling urban center. Then in 1500, the Indigenous tribes of the Illini Confederation, after which the state is named, arrived. They thrived until the French colonized the area in the 1600s. The British followed and soon claimed Illinois as their own. It wasn't until 1818 that Illinois became the 21st state of America.

Today, Illinois is known as the "Prairie State." It is the flattest state in the country and is 75% farmland. It has plenty of bragging rights, being the first state to abolish slavery, the first to build a skyscraper, and the first to have all-color TV. It also introduced the world to Ferris wheels, dishwashers, and zippers!

ROCKFORD · CHICAGO · NAPERVILLE · AURORA · JOLIET · SPRINGFIELD

ILLINOIS

28

SWEET TOOTHS
Chicago was at one time home to over 1,000 candy companies. It's the perfect place to satisfy sweet cravings!

POLISH TRIANGLE
Pick up some pierogi (filled dumplings) in the Polish Triangle. This area of Chicago boasts the most Polish-speakers outside of Poland.

ANIMAL PROTECTORS
The Lincoln Park Zoo is one of the nation's oldest public zoos, and one of its largest conservation programs.

DWYANE WADE
B.1982
13-time NBA All-Star whose foundation supports his hometown, Chicago, with community outreach programs.

SHONDA RHIMES
B.1970
First African American woman to create and produce a top network series, including one of Netflix's biggest shows to date, *Bridgerton*.

DIMA ELISSA
B.1963
CEO and founder of a company that designs and prints 3D body parts. She is an advocate for women in STEM and president of the organization Women In Bio Chicago.

NEAPOLITAN IMMIGRANTS
Immigrants from Naples, Italy, brought pizza to Chicago in the 1880s. Its deep-dish pizza is now world-famous.

FEEL THE BEAT!
Black DJs and music producers from Chicago created electronic dance music in the 1980s. Tracks typically have 120 to 130 beats per minute!

LITTLE PUERTO RICO
Paseo Boricua is known for its Puerto Rican residents. A 59-foot sculpture of the Puerto Rican flag and a walk of fame celebrate the thriving community.

GOSPEL MUSICIANS
Chicago is thought to be the birthplace of gospel, with roots in the music of West Africa. Chicago celebrates this blend of blues, jazz, and swing at its annual Gospel Music Festival.

WALT DISNEY
1901–1966
Famous pioneer of animation who revolutionized the entertainment industry with films, theme parks, and characters like Mickey Mouse.

ILLINOIS

THE RAVINIA MUSIC FESTIVAL
The Ravinia Music Festival is the oldest outdoor music event in America. The festival showcases a whole range of styles, from symphony to rock, and has included performances from artists like Louis Armstrong and Kenny Rogers and Maroon 5 and Lady Gaga. It also supports budding artists, hosting 60 of the world's top young musicians every year so that they can train and perform with the festival's headlining artists.

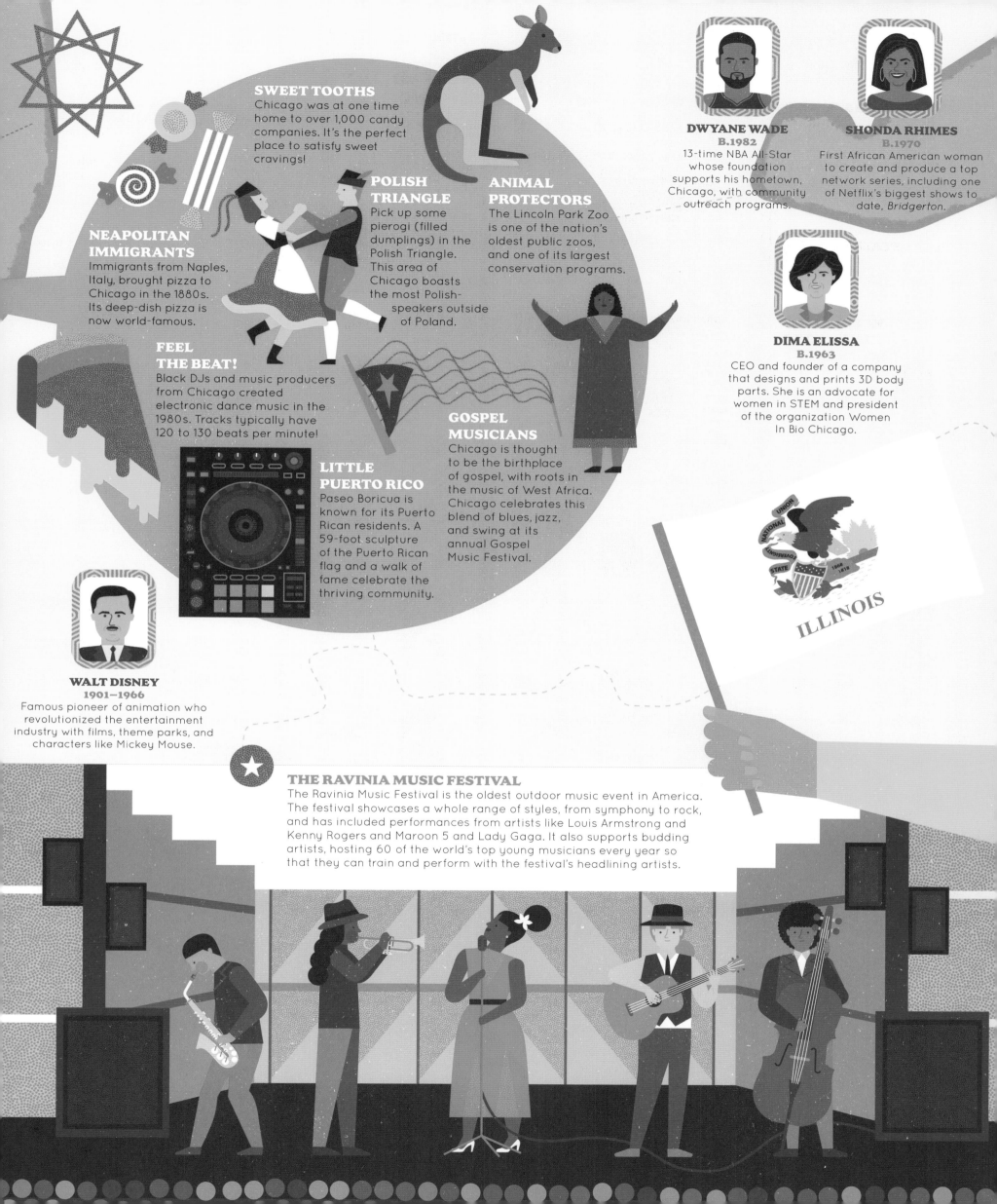

GERMAN HOOSIERS

Nearly a quarter of Indiana's population can claim German ancestry! Every year, a series of festivals throughout the state celebrates their heritage.

HOUSES ON WHEELS

Elkhart County is the RV capital of the World. It's where more than 80% of RVs are manufactured and it has an RV Hall of Fame.

CLASSIC CAR ENTHUSIASTS

The Auburn Cord Duesenberg Festival is known as the greatest classic car show in the world. It showcases some of the first automobiles ever made.

TENSKWATAWA, "THE PROPHET"
1775–1836
A leader of the Shawnee Tribe who, alongside his brother, Tecumseh, established a pan-Indigenous movement against invading white settlers.

SOUTH BEND

FORT WAYNE

BASEBALL'S CHAMPIONS

The first professional baseball game was played in Fort Wayne. Record-setting players like Barry Jones, Ron Kittle, and Lloyd McClendon have all come from Indiana.

ELWOOD HAYNES
1857–1925
Invented the first car powered by gasoline in 1894.

INTERSTATE INDIANA 64

HALL OF HEROES

In Elkhart superhero fans visit the world's only comic book and superhero museum.

SALLIE WYATT STEWART
1881–1951
Teacher who founded Evansville's first Inter-Racial Commission and several institutions to improve life for Black people.

ROAD TRIPPERS

The center of several major interstate highways, Indiana is known as "The Crossroads of America." Millions of people have passed through over the years!

BURMESE AMERICANS

Home to a large population of Burmese Chin refugees, Indianapolis is often called Chindianapolis. Its streets are lined with Asian stores and eateries.

VICE PRESIDENTS

In almost every election between 1868 and 1916 there was a "Hoosier" on the ballot. It earned Indiana the nickname, "Mother of Vice Presidents!"

CARMEL

RACE-CAR DRIVERS

Get ready to see some of the greatest race-car drivers at the world-famous Indy 500 race, where there is enough space to seat nearly half a million people.

MAICEL D. MALONE-WALLACE
B.1969
Track and field athlete who won gold on the 4 × 400 meter relay team at the 1996 Olympics.

ISNA

Muslim Hoosiers founded the Islamic Society of North America (ISNA) nearly 60 years ago. It is now the largest Muslim organization on the continent.

INDIANAPOLIS

GOLDFISH KEEPERS

Martinsville opened the first successful goldfish farm in America. They're experts at caring for goldfish and supply pet stores all over the U.S.

BLUEGRASS MUSICIANS

The Bean Blossom Bluegrass Festival is the oldest running bluegrass country music festival in the world.

KEY FACTS

CAPITAL CITY
Indianapolis

TOTAL POPULATION OF STATE
6,785,528

AREA OF STATE (SQ MI)
36,420

POPULATION OF CAPITAL
887,642

ALBINO ANIMALS

The longest navigable, underground river in the U.S. runs through Bluespring Caverns. It is an ideal habitat for blind and albino species like the northern cavefish, and may hold secrets to life-saving bacteria!

EVANSVILLE

FIRST PEOPLES

Angel Mounds dates back to the ancient Angel Chiefdom which was present around the year 1000 CE. At one point the town was occupied by more than 1,000 inhabitants.

WILBUR & ORVILLE WRIGHT
1867–1912 / 1871–1948
Wilbur Wright was born in Indiana and the two brothers invented and flew the world's first airplane in 1903.

INDIANA

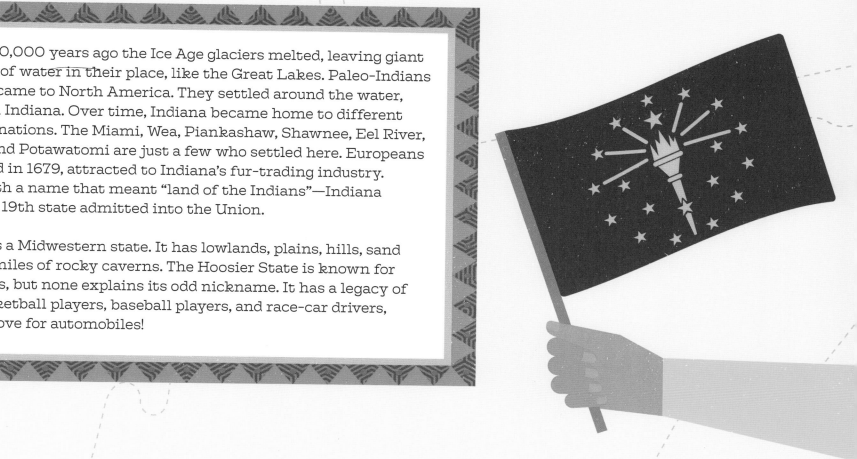

Some 10,000 years ago the Ice Age glaciers melted, leaving giant pools of water in their place, like the Great Lakes. Paleo-Indians then came to North America. They settled around the water, including in Indiana. Over time, Indiana became home to different Indigenous nations. The Miami, Wea, Piankashaw, Shawnee, Eel River, Delaware, and Potawatomi are just a few who settled here. Europeans then arrived in 1679, attracted to Indiana's fur-trading industry. In 1816—with a name that meant "land of the Indians"—Indiana became the 19th state admitted into the Union.

Indiana is a Midwestern state. It has lowlands, plains, hills, sand dunes, and miles of rocky caverns. The Hoosier State is known for many things, but none explains its odd nickname. It has a legacy of famous basketball players, baseball players, and race-car drivers, and a deep love for automobiles!

THE VALPARAISO POPCORN FESTIVAL

Indiana is a popcorn state! With corn being its top commodity, Hoosiers grow over 75,000 acres of the vegetable every year for popcorn alone. They celebrate the iconic snack at the Valparaiso Popcorn Festival. The festival includes crafts, food, fine art booths, and a running event called the Popcorn Panic. However, its most exciting attraction is a string of bands and popcorn-themed floats that make up the nation's one and only Popcorn Parade!

HOBO HISTORY
Britt locals keep "hobo" culture alive in this museum dedicated to crafts and teaching the adventurous side to traveling the country.

CHIEF

HOBO MUSEUM NOW OPEN

WIND POWER
Over 50% of Iowa's energy is produced by wind farms, making the state one of the leaders in renewable energy.

BIG BUSINESS
Iowa has a strong economy with several big businesses, like John Deere, Quaker Oats, and Heinz, employing thousands of people.

IRISH CULTURE
With Celtic dance and delicious Irish food, Iowans celebrate Irish culture annually in Waterloo.

WINTER GAMES
The often cold and icy winters don't stop Iowans! Residents participate in the annual Winter Games, competing in broomball, flag football, and even a chili cook-off.

SIOUX CITY

CEDAR RAPIDS

CYCLONE FANS
Iowans love their state school, Iowa State, and their Big 12 powerhouse football team, known as the Cyclones.

FOX LANGUAGE
This language is spoken by the Indigenous Meskwaki group around their settlement.

IOWA CITY

SIOUX CULTURE
The Yankton Sioux inhabited the area around Sioux City, which is known for its tallgrass prairies.

DES MOINES

FUTURE BIRTHPLACE OF
CAPTAIN JAMES T. KIRK
MARCH 22, 2228

TREKKIE'S PARADISE
Star Trek fans flock to Riverside, home to Captain James T. Kirk's birthplace monument, dated 2228.

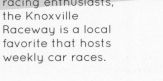

WESTERN ICON
Western fans visit Winterset to pay homage to the iconic John Wayne, the most popular Western film star in history.

SPEED RACERS
With a stadium that holds over 21,000 racing enthusiasts, the Knoxville Raceway is a local favorite that hosts weekly car races.

HISTORIC DAVENPORT
One of the largest Black communities in Iowa, Davenport is home to a lively community full of history.

CORN GROWERS
As the largest producer of corn in the nation, Iowa boasts that 97% of its farms are family owned.

KEY FACTS

CAPITAL CITY
Des Moines

TOTAL POPULATION OF STATE
3,190,369

AREA OF STATE (SQ MI)
56,273

POPULATION OF CAPITAL
214,133

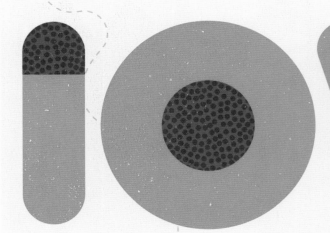

GERMAN MELODIES

With a strong German influence, Iowans still celebrate their German heritage with festivals and even singing groups.

ORGANIC FARMERS

Iowa ranks sixth in the nation for its number of organic farms—over 700 in total! It also runs a state association for gardeners, farmers, and advocates for healthy food.

DAVENPORT

K nown as the "Heartland of America," Iowa is a prairie state filled with farmland that nourishes the nation. The area now called Iowa came under U.S. control after the Louisiana Purchase in 1803, and opened up for settlement in 1833. It became a state in 1846. German and Irish immigrants flocked to the new state but were shocked by its geography. Settlers had to learn how to manage the grand prairies by setting occasional fires to prevent the grass and bush from overtaking the area. Soon, they learned how to manage the land and created vast stretches of farmland for crops like corn and soybeans.

For years, farmers were the heart of Iowa. At the annual Iowa State Fair—one of the largest in the country—the agricultural contest always draws a crowd. The mass farms attracted big businesses and new technology. You'll also find acres of wind farms, as Iowans move toward creating more renewable energy. Today, Iowa is a great destination full of cozy towns, scenic views, and fertile farmland.

LOLO JONES
B.1982
An award-winning hurdler and bobsledder, Jones won a World Championship as a bobsledder in 2021.

NATASHA KAISER-BROWN
B.1967
A national collegiate champion, Brown is known for her achievement in track and field.

ELIJAH WOOD
B.1981
This busy actor is known for playing the iconic hero, Frodo Baggins, in *The Lord of the Rings*.

DANAI GURIRA
B.1978
This popular actor, born in Grinnell, is also a Tony Award-nominated playwright.

KURT WARNER
B.1971
A former NFL quarterback, Warner is a Super Bowl Most Valuable Player.

THE FARM STATE

Iowa is important to the nation because of its farms. As a farm state, Iowa is one of the top corn and soybean producers. These are staples of many foods, such as ketchup, cereal, and more. State residents also lead the way in raising hogs and cattle. In fact, Iowans raise more hogs than any other state. While Iowa looks to the future with renewable energy, many residents have not forgotten their farm roots—and thankfully so! Without the great farmers of Iowa, America wouldn't enjoy the easy access it has to some of its most popular food.

REACH FOR THE STARS

Residents of Hutchinson have all the reason to reach for the stars. The Cosmosphere, a haven for STEM enthusiasts and space lovers, is located there. Locals and visitors can learn more about science and the history of space exploration. The building houses a planetarium, exhibit gallery, classrooms, and a theater. With over 35,000 square feet of science fun, residents of all ages can stargaze and participate in interactive sessions. Nestled in the grand plains of Kansas, this center aims to inspire Kansan youth to become tomorrow's STEM leaders.

HENRY PERRY
1874–1940
Known as the father of Kansas City barbecue, Perry's unique cooking style attracted people from all over, and birthed delicious sauces that helped Kansas City become a barbecue hotspot.

NINA E. ALLENDER
1873–1957
One of the earliest advocates of women's rights, Allender drew attention to women's suffrage at a time when women did not have the right to vote.

HATTIE McDANIEL
1893–1952
A talented actor, McDaniel was the first African American to win an Oscar for acting.

GWENDOLYN BROOKS
1917–2000
This famous poet and author became the first African American to win a Pulitzer Prize.

HISTORIC TOWN
The town of Nicodemus is the only remaining Midwestern town founded by African Americans after the Civil War and is home to around 14 residents.

BIRD WATCHERS
Over 335 species of bird have been documented in Cheyenne Bottoms basin. Bird enthusiasts visit this 41,000-acre marshland to get a peek of the diverse bird species.

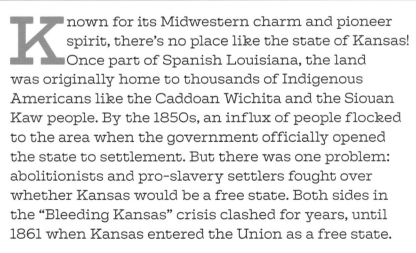

Known for its Midwestern charm and pioneer spirit, there's no place like the state of Kansas! Once part of Spanish Louisiana, the land was originally home to thousands of Indigenous Americans like the Caddoan Wichita and the Siouan Kaw people. By the 1850s, an influx of people flocked to the area when the government officially opened the state to settlement. But there was one problem: abolitionists and pro-slavery settlers fought over whether Kansas would be a free state. Both sides in the "Bleeding Kansas" crisis clashed for years, until 1861 when Kansas entered the Union as a free state.

The region was brought to the forefront of history in a landmark case that finally made segregation in all schools illegal in the early 1950s. Years later, Kansas is an inclusive state attracting diversity in industry, education, and agriculture. Today, Kansans enjoy the Great Plains, beautiful sunflower fields, and a dynamic history.

KANSAS COWBOYS
Folks in Kansas love a good rodeo! Residents in Garden City host a national three-day rodeo that celebrates the Old West.

GORDON PARKS
1912–2006
Chronicling African American life with photos through the 1940s to 1970s, Parks was the first African American to produce big-budget movies.

Kansas

MURAL ARTISTS
Like China, Topeka has its own Great Wall—and it's covered in vibrant images of the city's history, painted by local artists.

KICKAPOO LAND
In 1832, the Kickapoo Tribe of Kansas was relocated to a reservation covering 150,000 acres of land near the Missouri River.

STORM CHASERS
Kansas is one of the most tornado-prone states. Weather enthusiasts and storm chasers flock to the area to track and learn more about these dangerous weather patterns.

GERMANFEST
With a large population of residents with German roots, Topeka is the home of the annual Germanfest, an annual celebration of German culture that is 45 years old.

EXODUSTERS
With a population of less than 10%, many Black Kansans trace their lineage back to the Exodusters. This is a group of African Americans who migrated to Kansas from the Deep South during the late 19th century

FOOTBALL FANS
Football fanatics go wild in Kansas! With nearly 50,000 roaring fans, the Kansas State Wildcats are one of the state's most popular teams.

LOOSE MEAT FOODIES
One of the state's favorite meals is the loose meat sandwich, with its unpacked ground meat in two buns—you'll find it in local restaurants or at a neighbor's home for lunch!

KANSAS CITY

TOPEKA

OVERLAND PARK

OLATHE

SMOKY VALLEY CULTURE
Every other year the community in Lindsborg get together to celebrate Swedish culture. With music and education, this community keeps their heritage alive!

CATTLE FARMERS
The great plains state has many farms, but cattle estates take the lead, with over 27,000 farms.

WICHITA

ASIAN APPRECIATION
The Wichita Asian Association provides resources and events to teach people about the vibrant Asian culture in the area and throughout the world.

ICEE ICEE BABY!
Kansans love a sweet treat, and the state is home to one of the nation's favorite frozen drinks—the ICEE!

MEDIEVAL MERRIMENT
Residents in Wichita enjoy the Great Plains Renaissance and Scottish Festival, where the community celebrates history and culture with knights, knaves, and bagpipes!

KEY FACTS

CAPITAL CITY
Topeka

TOTAL POPULATION OF STATE
2,937,880

AREA OF STATE (SQ MI)
82,278

POPULATION OF CAPITAL
126,587

KENTUC

WALNUT ST.

PICKUP TRUCKS

While many Southern folks enjoy the ease of pickup trucks, Kentuckians love to take to the road—and mud—in their trusty pickups that can haul four-wheelers and speed boats from place to place.

COVINGTON

ROOTS 101

In Louisville, the Roots 101 African American Museum showcases the rich culture and history of Black people in Kentucky.

THE COLONEL'S CHICKEN

Kentucky Fried Chicken is headquartered in Louisville. It was founded in 1930 by Colonel Harland Sanders, whose face forms the restaurant's iconic logo.

FRANKFORT

LEXINGTON

WALNUT MEMORIES

The historic Walnut Street was once a hub for the Louisville Black community, with 150 Black-owned businesses.

JUMPING JOCKEYS

The world's best jockeys, mostly from Puerto Rico, Panama, and Mexico, flock to Louisville to race in the Kentucky Derby. It is America's biggest horse race, and one of its oldest.

BIG SLUGGERS

The Louisville Slugger Museum opened in 1996. It is named after the style of baseball bat used by hall-of-famers like Babe Ruth.

HORSE HATS!

Wearing a big, colorful hat to the Kentucky Derby is a tradition that was popularized in the 1960s to bring good luck, and make a fashion statement.

LOUISVILLE

MARVELOUS MOONBOWS

Cumberland Falls is a popular waterfall that attracts locals and visitors for one very cool reason: moonbows! Moonbows are rainbows that take place at night, under the Moon.

OWENSBORO

TIME FOR TRACTORS

With over 76,000 farms, Kentucky residents need the best equipment. The Paducah Antique Gas Engine & Tractor Show is an annual event suited for tractor lovers and the whole family. It showcases tractors, small engines, and pulls that farmers love!

BOWLING GREEN

QUICK DELIVERY

One of the top delivery services in the world, United Parcel Services Airlines, or UPS, has its airport hub based in Louisville and employs over 20,000 people.

BLUEGRASS BANDS

A mix of Southern roots and Appalachian culture make bluegrass the hot sound in the state! With so many friendly towns, you'll catch a local band or two playing those twangy grooves.

KEY FACTS

CAPITAL CITY
Frankfort

TOTAL POPULATION OF STATE
4,505,836

AREA OF STATE (SQ MI)
40,409

POPULATION OF CAPITAL
28,602

PAMELA BROWN
B.1983
A television reporter and newscaster, Brown is known for her work on popular stations ABC and CNN.

BLACK INDEPENDENCE DAY

Enslaved Black people in Western Kentucky celebrated their emancipation on August 8th, 1868, which is different from the Juneteenth celebration in other areas of the country. Today, the day is still honored and celebrated.

ROLLIN' ON THE RIVER!

The Belle of Louisville is the oldest operating Mississippi River-style steamboat navigating the Ohio River. Locals and visitors love to take the easy and nostalgic route it offers along the water.

WIRED WORKERS

General Cable is one of the world's largest wire and cable manufacturers, with a 170-year history. This historic company in Highland Heights has employed thousands over the years.

COAL MINERS

Kentucky is well known for its coal mining industry, with over 9,000 coal miners employed across the state as of 2015.

TINASHE
B.1993
Singer and actor Tinashe is known for her rhythmic voice and roles on popular shows like *Two and a Half Men.*

Known as the "Bluegrass State," Kentucky is home to horse racing, baseball bats, and Southern flair! The vast grassy lands of Kentucky were initially home to the Haudenosaunee and Sioux, among other Indigenous Americans. In 1792, Kentucky split from Virginia and was admitted into the Union. Like many Southern states, Kentucky gained its fortune from tobacco plantations worked by enslaved people. Once slavery was outlawed, Kentucky set out to make a new name for itself. It became notorious for its "blue grass," a type of grass that was popular with thoroughbred horses and led to statewide horse training and eventually racing.

Today, Kentucky has a history of many contributions to the United States. It's fourth in automobile production, employs over 4,000 soldiers and civilians at the historic Fort Knox, and is responsible for producing more than 20% of the country's electricity. The culture is a mix of Southern, Midwest, and Appalachian heritage. With the Appalachian Mountains to the east, Midwest influence, and Southern charm, over four million unique people call old Kentucky home.

GEORGE C. WOLFE
B.1954
An award-winning playwright, Wolfe was born in Frankfort and went on to Los Angeles and Broadway, becoming an iconic writer, director, and producer.

bell hooks
1952–2021
Author, feminist, and activist, hooks was known for her work centering Black women and their experiences.

PHILLIP ALLEN SHARP
B.1944
Nobel Prize-winner for advancing research on cancer and hereditary diseases.

THE MUHAMMAD ALI CENTER

Born in Louisville, from an early age Muhammad Ali had a fire in him for standing up for his beliefs and fighting with passion. Known for his outgoing personality and outstanding athleticism in the boxing ring, Ali became a hero who spoke out about the unequal treatment of Black people in America. The Muhammad Ali Center is a museum dedicated to his life and legacy. You'll find dramatic presentations, videos, interactive exhibits, and artifacts that teach about Ali's impact on the world. Folks who want to be inspired by "The Greatest," and how he used his platform to promote social justice and peace, will enjoy learning about one of America's most distinguished icons.

MUHAMMAD ALI CENTER

DON LEMON
B.1966
A Baton Rouge native, Lemon is an award-winning journalist known for his coverage of Hurricane Katrina.

MADAM C. J. WALKER
1867–1919
Born Sarah Breedlove, this self-made millionaire created hair products for African Americans.

EMERIL LAGASSE
B.1959
Award-winning chef and media personality. He is a master of Creole- and Cajun-inspired food.

DJ KHALED
B.1975
This award-winning music producer and best-selling author started off as a DJ in New Orleans.

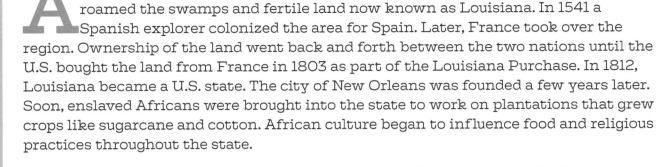

About 12,000 years ago, the ancestors of today's Indigenous American groups roamed the swamps and fertile land now known as Louisiana. In 1541 a Spanish explorer colonized the area for Spain. Later, France took over the region. Ownership of the land went back and forth between the two nations until the U.S. bought the land from France in 1803 as part of the Louisiana Purchase. In 1812, Louisiana became a U.S. state. The city of New Orleans was founded a few years later. Soon, enslaved Africans were brought into the state to work on plantations that grew crops like sugarcane and cotton. African culture began to influence food and religious practices throughout the state.

Today, the region boasts Indigenous, French, Canadian, Spanish, and African influences. This mix creates Louisiana's unique culture. Louisiana attracts people from all over the world because of its festivals, music, and distinctive food. Louisiana is known as a state bursting with culture.

TUNICA-BILOXI TRIBE
The Tunica-Biloxi Tribe hosts an annual powwow where they teach visitors about their culture and traditions.

LOUISIANA CREOLES
Influenced by French, Spanish, and African ancestry, Creole culture can be found in south Louisiana, New Orleans, and Natchitoches.

CHITIMACHA TRIBE
The first inhabitants of the Mississippi River Delta, the Chitimacha, continue to craft their world-famous baskets.

THE COUSHATTA
The Coushatta people are known for their large gaming casino and contributions to Louisiana culture.

SUGAR CANE FARMERS
One of the top producers of sugar cane in the United States, most farms are in south Louisiana.

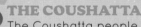

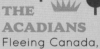

ZYDECO DANCERS
Zydeco dance style is performed by people in Acadiana. Couples dance together to rhythmic music accompanied by an accordion.

THE ACADIANS
Fleeing Canada, the Acadian people settled in southwestern Louisiana in 1764. The area is now nicknamed "Acadiana."

BATON ROUGE

THE HOUMA
This Indigenous American group represents over 17,000 people and has a major city named after them.

LAFAYETTE

CRAWFISH CAPITAL

Breaux Bridge, a small town in Louisiana, is known for its little red crustaceans called crawfish. These edible creatures pack a lot of flavor and are a popular dish throughout the state. Breaux Bridge is known as the "Crawfish Capital of the World." It hosts an annual festival to celebrate local dishes such as the Cajun-inspired crawfish *étouffée*, a "smothered" dish served with rice. From fried crawfish to spicy boiled crawfish paired with corn and potatoes, the annual crawfish festival is a regional favorite that explores this tasty cuisine.

CARNIVAL CROWDS

Nearly 1.4 million people attend Mardi Gras in New Orleans every year. People across the state celebrate with colorful parades.

CEMETERY TOURISTS

New Orleans is below sea level, so many people are buried above ground in marble chambers. These "cities of the dead" are sacred to the area.

HAITIAN HERITAGE

Today, Haitian influence can be seen in the shotgun style houses and religious practices around Orleans parish.

MAGICAL MUSICIANS

Musicians enjoy special festivals throughout the state and in art districts like Treme or the French Quarter.

COOL KREWES

During Mardi Gras, organizations sponsor parades called krewes. They build big, colorful floats that cruise down parade routes.

AFRICAN HERITAGE

In the 19th century, enslaved people gathered weekly at Congo Square. Today, tourists visit the area and listen to lively music.

ALLIGATOR HUNTERS

With about two million wild alligators, many people make a living hunting for alligators in the swamp areas.

UNION JUSTICE CONFIDENCE

QUVENZHANE WALLIS
B. 2003

After starring in her first movie at five years old, this award-winning actor is also a children's book author. She also made history by becoming the first Black girl to star in a remake of the classic film, *Annie*.

KEY FACTS

CAPITAL CITY
Baton Rouge

TOTAL POPULATION OF STATE
4,657,757

AREA OF STATE (SQ MI)
52,378

POPULATION OF CAPITAL
227,470

39

STEPHEN KING
B.1947
Best-selling author of horror and supernatural fiction novels, who often uses Maine as the setting of his novels.

PERCY LEBARON SPENCER
1894–1970
Physicist and inventor of the microwave oven, born in Howland.

IAN LOWELL CROCKER
B.1982
Swimming world champion with five Olympic medals.

FATIMA DARLING GRIFFIN
1806–1890
A free Black woman who founded Maine's first mixed-race community on Malaga Island in the 1860s. The islanders inspired hope for racial equality in Maine.

GRAFFITI ARTISTS
Battery Steele was a World War II military fort. Its tunnels are claimed by artists during the annual Sacred and Profane festival.

SUDANESE MAINERS
Portland is home to one of the oldest and largest communities of Sudanese Americans, and is the most diverse city in Maine!

SCI-FI ENTHUSIASTS
The International Cryptozoology Museum houses fossils of Bigfoot and the Loch Ness Monster, plus hair samples of Abominable Snowmen.

ECCENTRIC COLLECTION
The Umbrella Cover Museum holds a Guinness World Record for its quirky collection of discarded umbrella covers.

FREE AFRICAN AMERICANS
The Abyssinian Meeting House is Maine's oldest Black church. It was a safehouse for people escaping from slavery, and a hub for Black life and culture for over 80 years.

HIGH HIKERS
The 5,268-foot Mount Katahdin is Maine's tallest mountain. Its wild Knife Edge Trail draws adventurous hikers from all over.

LUCKY SAILORS
Even experienced sailboat captains can get caught in Old Sow, one of the largest and most dangerous whirlpools on the planet.

ICE FISHERMEN
Trout season never ends in Maine, but ice fishing is what it's famous for! This most popular of fish species can be caught practically anywhere along Maine's lengthy shoreline.

BERRY PICKERS
Maine is the largest producer of wild blueberries in the world!

BANGOR

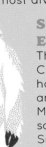

DOROTHEA LYNDE DIX
1802–1887
Groundbreaking American activist who fought for the rights of people with mental illnesses.

LOBSTERING
Maine lobster is one of the oldest continuously run industries in North America, dating back to the 1600s. Maine's lobstermen catch 80% of America's lobsters!

AUGUSTA

LEWINSTON

THE SHAKERS
The last active community of Shakers, a Christian sect, is based in New Gloucester.

WHALE WATCHERS
Maine's 3,500-mile tidal coastline is one of the longest in America. Its waters bustle with whales, including humpbacks, finbacks, minkes, and more.

PORTLAND

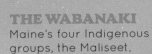

THE WABANAKI
Maine's four Indigenous groups, the Maliseet, Micmac, Penobscot, and Passamaquodd, also known as the Wabanaki, are celebrated at the Abbe Museum and around the state in unique ways, like the Wabanaki Canoe Trip.

BIDDEFORD

ICE AGE HUNTERS
The Maine Ice Age Trail explores ancient hunters' trails of mountains, cliffs, and lakes, which were carved by gigantic glaciers that melted over millions of years.

SANFORD

MOVIEMAKERS
Movies like *Forrest Gump*, *Jumanji*, *Lake Placid*, and *The Cider House Rules* were shot in Maine, a hotspot for film production.

maine

KEY FACTS

CAPITAL CITY
Augusta

TOTAL POPULATION OF STATE
1,362,359

AREA OF STATE (SQ MI)
35,380

POPULATION OF CAPITAL
18,899

The first inhabitants of the land now called Maine were hunters from the Ice Age. Years later, the Wabanaki Confederacy of five Indigenous nations lived in the region. In the 1600s, the French settled in the area and a century later, the British arrived. Maine officially became a U.S. state in 1820. It was the 23rd to be admitted to the Union and one of the few established as an anti-slavery state. Also called the "Pine Tree State," it is today sparsely populated. However, it's a hotspot for tourists in New England.

A total of 90% of the region is covered in forests, and it has over 4,000 offshore islands, including cliffs and hills partially submerged from melting Ice Age glaciers. Maine is the home of the nation's largest moose population, and also the nation's main source of lobsters, wild blueberries, and toothpicks!

★ LOBSTER BOAT RACING
The century-old tradition of lobster boat racing is less about winning —since lobster boats are designed to fish, not to go fast! It's more about celebrating the lobster industry that helps keep Maine afloat.

SUBMARINE RACES

A massive swimming pool in Bethesda is home to high-tech human-powered submarine competitions, known as the International Submarine Races. Run by the Naval Surface Warfare Center since 1989, this race is all fun and no business! It also aims to introduce students to STEM careers by having them learn from top naval scientists. The race features two dozen teams with different designs, all somehow human-powered.

RUTH BLEIER
1923-1988

A feminist scientist who raised awareness of sexism in biology, Bleier was committed to social justice for women and the poor.

TONI BRAXTON
B.1967

A woman of many talents—singer, songwriter, pianist, actress—Braxton has sold over 70 million records and is one of the best-selling female artists ever.

DR. TERESA COHEN
1892-1992

A Baltimore native, Cohen was a mathematician and the first woman to join the math department at Pennsylvania State University.

MOUNTAIN CULTURE

The Appalachian community of Western Maryland is home to famous apple orchards and dairy cattle farms. The farmers and rural community help keep the state's economy going.

JESSICA WATKINS
B.1988

A NASA astronaut, aquanaut, and former rugby player, Watkins has won many awards for her planetary research and inspires a generation of girls to pursue STEM careers.

Known for its great seafood and diverse people, Maryland is full of strong tradition and dynamic culture. This coastal area was home to Algonquin people before it was taken over by Europeans. Soon after, the area known as Maryland became one of the original 13 states.

During the Civil War, freedom seekers used a system of safe passages through Maryland to gain liberation. As the 20th century approached, Maryland became a hub of manufacturing and shipping during the Industrial Revolution.

Today, Maryland households are the wealthiest in the country. The economy, once dependent on farming, now leads in jobs in technology, defense, and science. With the most historic landmarks in the country, and a continuously growing tech industry, Maryland is a state that attracts people from all over to its bustling communities.

M

KEY FACTS

CAPITAL CITY
Annapolis

TOTAL POPULATION OF STATE
6,177,224

AREA OF STATE (SQ MI)
12,406

POPULATION OF CAPITAL
40,812

HAIRSPRAY!
Hairspray, the famous Broadway play and movie, brings theater-lovers from around the world to the city that inspired songs such as "Good Morning Baltimore!"

ETHIOPIAN AMERICANS
Baltimore's historic Chinatown has a growing Ethiopian population. There are over 75,000 Ethiopian Marylanders.

NAIJA INFLUENCE
Nigerians in Baltimore host the annual Naija Fest to celebrate their heritage.

CHARMED, I'M SURE
Baltimore is full of street art and attractions like the Visionary Art Museum. It is also the site of poet Edgar Allan Poe's house. There is always something interesting to see or do in "Charm City!"

CHRISTMAS MIRACLES
Since the 1940s, Hampden has had an entire street of homes adorned with Christmas decorations. Known as the Miracle on 34th Street, this tradition keeps locals and visitors excited about the holiday season.

LUMBEE TRIBE
Originally from the North Carolina area, the Lumbee migrated to Maryland and formed a community. Today, the Baltimore American Indian Center showcases Lumbee art and culture.

BLACK ICONS
Baltimore is home to some of the most significant figures in Black American history—in wax form! The National Great Blacks In Wax Museum features lifesized sculptures of Black icons like Malcolm X, Billie Holiday, and President Barack Obama.

HISTORIC KOREAN COMMUNITIES
The Baltimore-Washington metro area is home to the third largest Korean population in the country, dating back to the 20th century. Koreatown was officially opened in 2021 in Ellicott City, to honor this thriving community.

KOREATOWN

BALTIMORE

COLUMBIA

GERMANTOWN

REAL CRABBY PATTIES
Maryland folks love their crabs! From crab cakes to boiled crab, the state has made a name from all things crab. They mix it with Old Bay Seasoning—the perfect pairing!

NAVY LOVE
Annapolis is home to the second oldest of the country's five service academies, the Navy. During the annual U.S. Army vs Navy game, Maryland residents root for the Navy—always—and are huge supporters of the local cadets and academy.

ANNAPOLIS

SILVER SPRING

SNOWBALLS FOR ALL!
Maryland residents love snowballs! While shaved ice and tasty, sweet flavor is found in many places, snowballs in this state are the essential summer treat!

HISPANIC CULTURE
Representing over 10% of the state's population, Hispanic and Latino residents have a lively community in Montgomery county and a strong culture across the state.

LACROSSE LOVERS
Nicknamed the "Heartland of Lacrosse," Maryland residents love lacrosse and have made it the state team sport! From toddlers to college players, residents grow up playing and cheering for their home teams!

BILLIE HOLIDAY
1915–1959
Best known for her stirring song, "Strange Fruit", Holiday used her voice to protest the injustices Black people faced.

WALDORF

RUN FOR IT!
Athletes in Maryland have many races and marathons to look forward to. One of the most active states, Maryland has a race for every running level, and even has running festivals!

MARYLAND

MOROCCAN FESTIVALS

Revere is home to a growing Moroccan diaspora. The Moroccan community celebrates its heritage with festivals around the state. Revere hosts the largest in the region! The colorful displays of food, music, henna, and crafts allow everyone a glimpse of Morocco, all without leaving the Bay State.

BRAZILIAN AMERICANS

Historic Portuguese-speaking communities have made central Massachusetts a hub for Brazilian Americans. The Brazilian Independence Day Festival is the largest gathering for New England's Brazilian community.

SHREWSBURY INDIAN AMERICANS

Shrewsbury and the 495/Metrowest Corridor are home to a budding community of Indian Americans. The new locals share their culture through celebrations of Diwali and Holi, as well as an annual India Day.

THE MASSACHUSETT NATION

The Massachusett were present when the English invaded, and their nation gives the state its name. They still live in communities throughout Massachusetts.

MOSWETUSET HUMMOCK

LOWELL

CAMBRIDGE

BOSTON

WORCESTER

LITTLE KAMPALA

Waltham has been a center for Ugandan culture since the 1960s. It continues to welcome Ugandan students and immigrants with eateries, religious organizations, radio stations, and more.

VOLLEYBALL STARS

Holyoke is where volleyball was invented, in 1895. Its International Volleyball Hall of Fame honors players, coaches, and officials.

PANCAKE LOVERS

Springfield serves up the world's largest pancake breakfast! To celebrate the city's founding, a festival is held with a giant pancake menu.

SPRINGFIELD

DR. SEUSS FANS

Springfield was the home of Theodor Geisel: the famous Dr. Seuss! A museum in town is dedicated to his colorful universe of quirky books.

BLACK BOSTONIANS

Roxbury, one of Boston's oldest neighborhoods, has been the state's center for Black art, culture, and community for decades. Malcolm X lived here as a teenager. It is the site of the city's first urban farms and New England's largest mosque.

MASSACHUSETTS

ELIZABETH WARREN
B.1949
The first woman elected to serve Massachusetts in the U.S. Senate, famous for her fight for economic equality.

JAMES NAISMITH
1861–1939
The Springfield gym teacher who invented basketball in 1891.

SYRIA TOWN
Syrian and Lebanese people have lived here since at least 1880. They helped renew Boston and develop its first thriving Arab American hub.

CHINESE BAY STATERS
Boston has one of America's largest Chinatowns. The first known Chinese person in America, Zhou Libei, is buried here. Boston celebrates Chinese culture with an epic New Year parade, filled with lion dancers, drums, firecrackers, and delicious food.

ITALIANS IN BOSTON
Since the early 1900s, Italian Bostonians have been celebrating their culture, food, and art with festivals like the Fisherman's Feast, which leads a parade to Boston Harbor.

For more than 10,000 years, various tribes of the Wampanoag people have lived in present-day Massachusetts, later joined by the Narragansett, Abenaki, Nipmuc, and others. Starting in the late 1400s, Europeans began arriving on the Massachusetts shores, including the Pilgrim Fathers who took Plymouth in 1620.

In 1788, Massachusetts became the sixth American state. Nicknamed for its watery coasts, the Bay State has a unique history. It was the first region to establish and, then abolish slavery outright, the first to write and adopt a constitution, and the first to establish a university: Harvard. It's also the site of the first American subway, public park, school, and post office. It's famous for inventions such as the sewing machine and chocolate-chip cookies among other things.

Bay Staters come from everywhere. Massachusetts has always been a center for immigration. It has some of the largest communities of Moroccans, Brazilians, Ugandans, Italians, Irish, Chinese, Lebanese, Syrians, and Indians in America!

SETTLING FOR SEAWEED
Scituate is the most Irish town in the country. The first Irish immigrants discovered carrageenan, a substance used in many foods, in Scituate's seaweed. This "Irish moss" was used to make food, paint, and cosmetics.

PIRATE WRECK
The Whydah Pirate Museum in Yarmouth claims the world's largest collection of real pirate treasure recovered from a single shipwreck! The *Whydah* was a pirate ship that sank near Cape Cod, where its treasures were discovered centuries later.

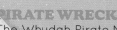

QUINCY MUSLIMS
The region's earliest Muslim community formed around 1875, when Lebanese and Syrian immigrants worked the local shipyards. Eight families in Quincy Point laid the roots for New England's first mosque.

THE MASHPEE WAMPANOAGS
This tribe built the Old Indian Meeting House on Cape Cod—the earliest Indigenous church in the east. It reflects an important history of forced conversion but also of community. African Americans married Wampanoags here, and supported their efforts to reclaim their rights.

TISQUANTUM (SQUANTO)
C. 1585–1662
A member of the Patuxet tribe who, after being enslaved by the English, escaped to Plymouth to act as a peace broker for the surviving Indigenous communities.

STEVE CARELL
B.1962
Award-winning comedian and actor born in Concord.

KEVIN SYSTROM
B.1938
Holliston-born tech entrepreneur, famous for co-founding Instagram.

KEY FACTS

CAPITAL CITY
Boston

TOTAL POPULATION OF STATE
7,029,917

AREA OF STATE (SQ MI)
10,554

POPULATION OF CAPITAL
675,647

MICHIGAN

SOJOURNER TRUTH
C.1797–1883
A formerly enslaved person, Truth became an outspoken advocate for abolition, temperance, and civil and women's rights.

MADONNA
B.1958
Best-selling female music artist of all time, known as the "Queen of Pop."

SID MEIER
B.1954
Programmer and designer, also called the "Father of Computer Gaming."

SERENA WILLIAMS
B.1981
This tennis legend has won an astonishinig 23 Grand Slams in her 20-plus-year career.

The word "Michigan" comes from an Ojibwe word meaning "large water." Ancestors of the Anishinaabeg or "original people" lived in the Great Lakes region known as Michigan nearly 13,000 years ago. Among the Anishinaabeg are the Ojibwe, Odawa, and Potawatomi nations, which in around 800 CE formed an alliance known as the Council of the Three Fires. The first Europeans arrived in Michigan in 1618—by accident. The French were searching for a route to China, but landed here instead. They colonized the land and began trading with local communities for furs. Then the British arrived and settled in Michigan for about a decade before the American Revolution. In 1837, it became the 26th state in the Union.

Today, Michigan is home to one of the largest Indigenous populations including 12 federally recognized and four state-recognized nations. It was one of the final stops along the Underground Railroad, the route to freedom for many enslaved people. It's also the birthplace of Motown music and an up-and-coming spot for fashion, theater, and food. It's known for many things including cars, copper, and wolverines!

BLACK EDEN
Idlewild was a thriving resort community founded in 1912. It was the premier holiday spot for Black Americans, including W.E.B. Du Bois, Madam C. J. Walker, and Aretha Franklin.

TREE GUARDIANS
The Michigan Society of American Foresters protects over 100 different tree species. They develop plans and systems to help grow and guard the forests.

THE HOPEWELL MOUNDS
More than 2,000 years ago the Hopewell people came to West Michigan. They built large, earthen mounds in which to bury their dead, with pottery, tools, jewelry, and other items. Today, 11 mounds still stand!

BLACK TASTEMAKERS
Black chefs and food entrepreneurs are shaping the way Detroit eats. Detroit has been reborn as a center for vegan food and unique blends of Black food flavors from around the world.

GRAND RAPIDS

LANSING

FANTASTIC FAIRIES
Fairyologists have "discovered" over two dozen, tiny, fairy doors in Ann Arbor! The fairies have a store and theater too.

ANN ARBOR

INVENTIVE MAGICIANS
Every year Colon hosts Abbott's Magic Get Together. Magicians from all over the world mingle to share their tricks and practice them on local people.

DINOSAUR LOVERS
Dinosaur Gardens is an abandoned attraction that contains a prehistoric forest, 15 life-size, fiberglass dinos, and a man-made volcano!

MICHIGAN'S GREAT MUSHROOMS

The fungal residents of Crystal Falls are arguably the largest living organisms on the planet. The "humongous fungus" covers 37 underground acres, weighs 21,000 pounds, and is around 1,500 years old. Oh, and it has its own festival: The Humongous Fungus Fest! People celebrate fungi with a tube float, fireworks, a fungus parade, and of course as the prized topping of the local Humongous pizza!

HIPPEWA HOPEWELL NCESTORS

chaeologists covered petroglyphs rved into rocks from tween 1,000 and 0 years ago. Local pes say the Sanilac troglyphs were eant to be guides for ure generations.

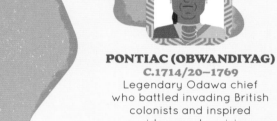

PONTIAC (OBWANDIYAG)
C.1714/20—1769
Legendary Odawa chief who battled invading British colonists and inspired a widespread uprising.

THE FIRST BOOK LENDERS
Michigan was the first state to protect libraries in its constitution! Its library system serves book-lovers at 651 locations.

FREEMASONS
The Freemasons are one of the oldest brotherhoods in the world. The world's largest Masonic Temple is in Detroit.

MOTORHEADS
Detroit is known as the "Car Capital of the World!" It's where Henry Ford invented the car assembly line to mass produce automobiles.

POST BY BOAT
Detroit has the U.S.'s only floating post office! The *J. W. Westcott II* is a boat that delivers mail to ships while they are afloat.

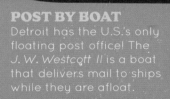

HITSVILLE, USA
Motown Records in Detroit was revolutionary. Its music broke down racial barriers, united people, and inspired today's pop and hip-hop artists. It produced legends like Stevie Wonder and The Supremes.

TECHTOWN CREATIVES
Detroit is a budding hub for building new technology. It is home to nearly 60,000 engineers!

STERLING HEIGHTS
WARREN
DETROIT

AMAZING MUSLIMS
Dearborn is the first Muslim-majority city in any state, home to the country's largest mosque, and the world's first museum of Arab American history.

KEY FACTS

CAPITAL CITY
Lansing

TOTAL POPULATION OF STATE
10,077,331

AREA OF STATE (SQ MI)
96,714

POPULATION OF CAPITAL
112,644

ICEBOX DAYS

The "Icebox of the Nation," International Falls celebrates the cold with its annual festival, Icebox Days. Events include frozen-turkey bowling, snow sculpting, cross-country skiing, and the famous race, Freeze Yer Gizzard Blizzard Run.

BEST PLACE TO RIDE

Minnesota has always been a cyclist's paradise, with over 250 miles of bike paths in Minneapolis alone.

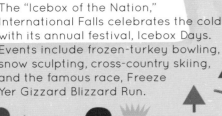

HALLOWEEN SPOOKS

Anoka is the "Halloween Capital of the World!" It is home to one of the oldest Halloween parades, which hosts haunting ghosts and ghouls.

HOCKEY PLAYERS

Minnesota is home to the U.S. Hockey Hall of Fame Museum. It also hosts the largest outdoor tournament on frozen water in the country!

PRINCE
1958–2016
One of the best-selling music artists of all time, who began gigging with his first band in Minneapolis.

DRED SCOTT
1799–1858
An enslaved African American man who unsuccessfully sued for his freedom in the *Scott* vs *Sandford* case in 1857. The Supreme Court's decision against Scott sparked fierce debate, and was an important event in the lead-up to the Civil War.

SOMALI AMERICANS

The Twin Cities are home to the largest Somali population in the U.S. In 2019, Somali American Ilhan Omar was elected as one of the first Muslim congresswomen.

THEATER BUFFS' DELIGHT

There are plenty of options for some drama in Minneapolis. The nation's oldest running theater, largest dinner theater, and largest regional playhouse are all in the city.

BOX OFFICE

DULUTH

WHERE TWO WATERS COME TOGETHER

The Bdote is where the Mississippi and Minnesota Rivers meet. For centuries it has held social, cultural, and historical significance for the Dakota, Ojibwe, enslaved people, and immigrants.

HMONG AMERICANS

St. Paul has the largest population of Hmong Americans. The first Hmong to arrive here were refugees from Laos in southeast Asia.

A FESTIVAL OF NATIONS

Minnesota hosts the longest-running multicultural festival in the Midwest. It celebrates over 100 ethnic groups from around the world, embracing cultural diversity.

JAPANESE OBON FESTIVAL

The Lantern Light Festival is an important Japanese holiday, during which the spirits of ancestors are believed to visit their families.

TRAILBLAZING DOCTORS

Minnesota has been the site of major medical breakthroughs in organ transplants, treatments for heart conditions, and pain relief.

SAINT PAUL

MINNEAPOLIS

BLOOMINGTON

ROCHESTER

PRINCE FANS

Visit music icon Prince's private estate and production complex, Paisley Park, to get a glimpse of his legendary creative universe.

JOY RIDES

Valleyfair is one of the largest amusement parks in the Midwest. It has more than 75 thrilling rides and eight loop-the-loop rollercoasters.

SHOP TILL YOU DROP

Super-shoppers from all over the world flock to the Mall of America in Bloomington, not only to shop, but to eat and play. It is the largest mall in the country and the size of 78 football fields!

CAVE EXPLORERS

Mystery Cave is the longest cave in the state carved by rushing water. Its 13 miles of underground passages are filled with stalactites, stalagmites, fossils, and underground pools.

ANN BANCROFT
B.1955
First woman recorded in history to cross the ice to the North Pole.

KEY FACTS

CAPITAL CITY
Saint Paul

TOTAL POPULATION OF STATE
5,706,494

AREA OF STATE (SQ MI)
86,936

POPULATION OF CAPITAL
311,527

BLACK LIVES MATTER

BLACK LIVES MATTER
While this movement began years earlier, it turned global with the killing of George Floyd by Minneapolis police in 2020. Nearly 26 million Americans marched to demand police accountability and reform, making this empowering movement one of the largest protests in U.S. history.

Indigenous groups have lived in Minnesota for around 12,000 years. By the 1600s, there were two main nations, the Dakota and the Ojibwe. In 1660, the French colonized their land. French influence declined after Thomas Jefferson bought the region in the Louisiana Purchase. Minnesota officially became the 32nd state in 1858.

Minnesota's nicknames include the "Gopher State," the "North Star State," and, most notably, the "Land of 10,000 Lakes." It has thousands of lakes and 92,000 miles of rivers and streams—enough to circle the planet nearly four times!

Minnesota is a place of great change but also great conflict. It was the first to elect Muslims to Congress, and became the center of the global Black Lives Matter movement in 2020. Its history also includes an impressive list of "firsts." Minnesotans invented the first water skis, toasters, and boxed cake mix, as well as seat belts, supercomputers, and heart surgery. They also have the world's largest pelican!

KEITH ELLISON
B.1963
First Muslim elected to Congress and first Black representative from Minnesota. As the state's attorney general, Ellison took on the George Floyd murder case in 2021.

JESSE JAMES
1847–1882
A notorious outlaw and legend of the Wild West, caught while robbing a bank in Northfield, Minnesota.

MINNESOTA

MISSISSIPPI

MOUND BAYOU
Jewel of The Delta
Est. 1887

DELTA BLUES
Blues lovers flock to the former home of blues greats like W. C. Handy and Muddy Waters. Clarksdale remains a historic marker for down-home music.

HBCU
Mississippi is home to six historically Black colleges and universities. Founded for Black students during segregation, these schools remain open to diverse students.

FREED SETTLERS
Mound Bayou is the oldest African American settlement founded by formerly enslaved people, which thrived despite Jim Crow laws that legitimized racism. Today, the area has a small but proud population.

SOUTHAVEN

WHERE THE BLUES WAS BORN
Dockery Plantation has been described as the birthplace of blues. Music lovers can visit the nearby Grammy Museum to celebrate the history and winners of the Grammy Awards.

DOCKERY FARMS
EST. 1895 BY
WILL DOCKERY 1865-1936
JOE RICE DOCKERY

FRIED FISH AND BLUES
Columbus is known for two things: fried fish and blues. Residents can eat while listening to great blues music in this historic area.

CHOCTAW NATION
Known for their strong business skills and livestock, the Mississippi Band of Choctaw are the only federally recognized nation in the state.

WINTERVILLE MOUNDS
The Winterville people are known for their unique pottery. Sacred mounds were created by this Indigenous American group in the area around 1450 CE.

CATFISH HEAVEN
As the "Catfish Capital of the World," Belzoni offers residents an abundance of farm-raised catfish and hosts an annual World Catfish Festival.

JACKSON

CROSSROADS QUILTERS
Keeping the tradition of quilting alive in their community, Black women in Port Gibson display and sell their unique handmade quilts at local shows.

BLACK FARMERS
In Mississippi, Black farmers account for a higher percentage of the total number of farmers than in any other state.

STUDENT ACHIEVERS
Piney Woods is the best known Black boarding school in the nation. Founded in 1909, students continue to attend the historic site for academic excellence.

HATTIESBURG

BILOXI

GULFPORT

KEY FACTS

CAPITAL CITY
Jackson

TOTAL POPULATION OF STATE
2,961,279

AREA OF STATE (SQ MI)
48,432

POPULATION OF CAPITAL
153,701

ROBIN ROBERTS
B. 1960
An award-winning journalist, Roberts was one of the first female sportscasters. She was inducted into the Women's Basketball Hall of Fame for her work in broadcasting.

ROY TUCKER
1951–2021

This stargazer is credited with the co-discovery of the near-Earth asteroid 99942 Apophis in 2004. He also discovered over 700 minor planets.

JOY BUOLAMWINI
B.1989

A Ghanaian American computer scientist, Buolamwini has won many awards for her work and is considered one of the world's greatest leaders in the field of science.

MYRLIE EVERS-WILLIAMS
B.1933

Williams became a civil rights activist and journalist who worked for 30 years seeking justice for her murdered husband, another civil rights activist.

BRANDY
B.1979

This famous singer made headlines as the first Black Cinderella on primetime television.

WRITERS TRAIL
Residents pay homage to Mississippi's great writers, like Angie Thomas and William Faulkner, by walking a guided trail with information about each writer.

HIGH STEPPIN' MUSICIANS
Known as one of the best marching bands in the land, Jackson State's Sonic Boom of the South is comprised of over 100 students from across the nation.

JOYFUL SINGERS
With over 100 members, the Mississippi Mass Choir is an award-winning gospel choir that began in 1988 in Jackson.

FREEDOM WALKERS
Starting in Jackson, the state's Freedom Trail has 25 markers across the region that tell the story of the people who contributed to the civil rights movement, and their struggle for freedom.

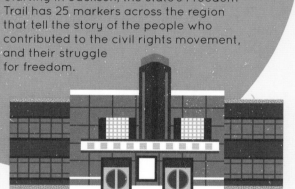

Mississippi has a deep-rooted history of Southern pride and tradition, and its residents are some of the most religious in America. Back in the 1800s, Mississippi was the nation's top cotton-producing state. The majority of people who lived in Mississippi at that time were enslaved. Enslaved people worked the vast cotton fields of large farms called plantations, and made the owners wealthy. Mississippi became a state in 1817 and was one of the seven original Confederate states.

Throughout the 20th century, most residents lived in rural areas and farming continued to be the dominant industry. As the years went by, Mississippi became known for its resistance to civil rights for African Americans. The hardships faced by the state's Black residents gave rise to a unique musical genre: the blues. In recent years, Mississippi has worked hard to correct its past mistakes. In 2021, it adopted a new flag to replace the controversial one that had flown for over 100 years and was a reminder of its infamous history. Featuring the region's beautiful magnolia flower, the new flag represents Mississippi's hope for a positive future and new traditions.

STICKBALL CHAMPIONS
For hundreds of years, stickball has been a major part of Choctaw life. Teams use handcrafted sticks and a woven leather ball. Mississippi Choctaw still participate in this historic game. Regional teams compete for a title and celebrate using tribal music and traditions. The goal of the competition is for members and visitors to immerse themselves in Choctaw culture and learn about their heritage. By keeping these traditions alive, the Choctaw spread awareness about their history and ways of life.

SUBTROPOLIS
Beneath Kansas City is the world's largest underground business complex, SubTropolis. It boasts 55 million square feet of businesses and storage.

BASEBALL HALL-OF-FAMERS
The Kansas City Monarchs were an all-Black baseball league during segregation, until 1962. Some of the players, such as Jackie Robinson, are now in the Baseball Hall of Fame.

MORMON BELIEVERS
The Mormons of Missouri have a rich history. The Kansas City Missouri Temple even won an award for its design.

SMOKEHOUSE DELIGHTS
Kansas City locals love their barbecue! You'll find smoked meats and sweet sauces amongst the many choices at specialty restaurants.

CAPITAL CITY
Jefferson City

TOTAL POPULATION OF STATE
6,154,913

AREA OF STATE (SQ MI)
69,707

POPULATION OF CAPITAL
43,228

GERMAN SETTLERS
Residents in the Missouri Rhineland area trace their roots back to German settlers who came to the state during the Industrial Revolution. Today, residents celebrate their German roots by hosting festivals that honor their food and traditions.

INDEPENDENCE

COLUMBIA

KANSAS CITY

ST. LOUIS

LICKETY-SPLIT!
Right in the center of Missouri is "Boone's Lick Country," hailed as the land where frontiersman Daniel Boone and his sons moved from Kentucky to trap game and make salt.

JEFFERSON CITY

SECRET SHELTER
Nearly 150,000 visitors a year walk through the limestone caverns that have been nestled in the Ozarks for 400 million years. They served as hideouts for many cultures throughout history.

DIVER'S HEAVEN
Divers flock to Bonne Terre for the world's largest man-made caverns, featuring 24 different swimming paths.

MAXINE WATERS
B.1938
With a career spanning over 40 years, Waters is one of the first African American women to be elected to the House of Representatives.

MISTY COPELAND
B.1982
This award-winning, twirling dancer is the first African American principal ballerina.

HEY! HAY! HAY!
The popular Ozark region is home to more than just beautiful scenery. Here, local farmers produce thousands of pounds of hay yearly, for the growing cattle industry.

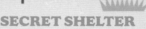

SPRINGFIELD

BAT PEOPLE
Ridgedale is home to a bat-filled cave with a bar, attracting residents to its weekly party scene. Talk about batty!

MISSOURI

DOROTHY VAUGHAN
1910–2008
This brainy mathematician and computer programmer was the first Black woman to manage an entire division of NASA.

LANGSTON HUGHES
1902–1967
Known as one of the leaders of the Harlem Renaissance, Hughes was a prolific writer and inventor of jazz poetry.

DR. HADIYAH-NICOLE GREEN
B.1981
A medical physicist known for the development of laser technology for treating cancer, Dr. Green has patented several therapies for cancer.

SYMPHONIC SOUNDS
With a popular music scene and timeless musicians, St. Louis is home to the second oldest U.S. orchestra.

TRAINS, PLANES, AND AUTOMOBILES
Many St. Louis residents work in the production of aerospace and transportation equipment. The state is home to around 100 aerospace production businesses.

MUSICAL MAYHEM
With a diverse musical history of jazz, blues, bluegrass, and country, St. Louis locals have their share of musical interests and legendary composers.

CHESS MATES
Folks who love a game of chess flock to St. Louis to learn tips and tricks about the game. They can also visit the World Chess Hall of Fame and learn about some of their favorite chess players.

CITY SLICKERS
Despite Missouri's Midwest charm, most of the population ditched the rural life for the city buzz. More than half of the state's population live in or near Kansas City or St. Louis.

Known as the "Show Me" state, Missouri residents like pointing that out! They don't just fall for anything; they have to see it to believe it. And this state has its share of things to see. The area known as Missouri has undergone many changes throughout the centuries. Before European settlers arrived, the land was occupied by the Osage and Missouria nations. Soon the French took control of the area spanning down to the Gulf of Mexico, and named it Louisiana. The land came under Spanish rule before finally becoming part of the United States in the Louisiana Purchase, and eventually a state in 1821. The area soon played a central role in westward expansion as a gateway to the west, while pioneer families from neighboring states flocked to the area and beyond.

Today, Missouri is a blend of Southern and Midwestern culture. Missourians are known for their delicious barbecue, jazz, and blues contributions. While residents stay true to their historic roots, finance also plays a major role in the state, with companies such as Wells Fargo, Edward Jones, and H&R Block headquartered here. Missouri is home to beautiful landscapes, epic scenery, and a courageous history.

BLACK AMERICANS AT ARROW ROCK
Right outside of Jefferson City is a historic community built by free and enslaved Black Americans. The Brown Lodge at Arrow Rock was built in 1881. The building now attracts hundreds of visitors for its exhibit chronicling the lives of the Black residents who were once enslaved on the land. Those residents became free, then sharecroppers and landowners. Eventually they left the area for better opportunities, but their roots remain. Today, with a population of only 56 people, Arrow Rock remains an important piece of the history of Black people in Missouri.

Brown Lodge
N 22

MONTANA

NATURE LOVERS' PARADISE

The Waterton-Glacier International Peace Park was founded as a symbol of good will between the U.S. and Canada. Both share management of one ecosystem that transcends borders, protecting the water, plants, and animals that make it a nature lovers' paradise.

WATERTON GLACIER INTERNATIONAL PEACE PARK

ALMA SMITH JACOBS
1916–1997
The first African American woman to serve as Montana State Librarian.

PHIL JACKSON
B.1945
A former professional basketball player considered to be one of the most successful coaches in NBA history.

VISIONARY BUDDHAS

Arlee's Garden of One Thousand Buddhas features 1,000 statues arranged to symbolize the cycle of death and rebirth central to Buddhism. The site is being constructed by volunteers, who hope that it will become a major place of worship for all faiths.

SALISH AND KOOTENAI TRIBES

The Flathead Indian Reservation is home to nearly 5,000 members of the Confederated Salish and Kootenai Tribes. The People's Center tells their story, through a museum, an exhibit gallery, and educational programs.

MISSOULA

HUTTERITE FARMERS

The Hutterite are a Christian group that believes in adult baptism and communal living. In Montana, they produce 90% of the state's hogs and 98% of its eggs.

GREAT FALLS

BIRDING HOTSPOTS

The organization Montana Audubon conserves wild spaces so native species like trumpeter swans, common loons, and nearly half a million snow geese can thrive.

LUGE RUNNERS

Lolo Hot Springs was where the first luge run was built in 1965. Montanans also made up most of the first U.S. Olympic luge team, hurling down the ice at super-high speeds!

HELENA

BUTTE-SILVER BOW

BOZEMAN

BILLINGS

AMERICA'S OLDEST CHINESE RESTAURANT

Pekin Noodle Parlor in Butte is the oldest continuously operating Chinese American restaurant in the country!

TREASURE HILL

Butte is called the "Richest Hill on Earth." During the Gold Rush in Montana, many immigrants came from Europe and China. It was also the birthplace of the American labor movement, protecting miners' rights and safety.

EVEL KNIEVEL DAYS

Butte—Evel Knievel's hometown—celebrates the daredevil's legacy every July with a free three-day sports festival, with races and stunts featuring motorcycles, BMX and mountain bikes, and skateboards.

GHOST TOWN

The famous ghost town Bannack was founded during the largest gold rush outside of California. Every year, on Bannack Days, people come together to re-enact pioneer life and celebrate mining history.

LIFESAVING POISON

Scientists at Berkeley Pit, a former copper mine, discovered that it is filled with deadly acidic water, heavy metals, and unique microscopic lifeforms. The new bacteria species evolved from the poisoned waters, and may help battle cancer.

BOOMING WILDLIFE

Conservationists at Yellowstone Wildlife Sanctuary rescue animals year-round, including bobcats, mountain lions, bison, eagles, wolves, elk, and black bears. No state has more mammals than Montana!

THE CROW FAIR AND RODEO

The Crow Fair and Rodeo is hosted by the largest reservation in Montana, the Crow Indian Reservation. The Crow Tribe has nearly 11,000 members, and for many, Crow is their first language. For over 100 years, they have organized the big Crow Fair, transforming the area into the "Teepee Capital of the World" and showcasing Crow Agency Dancers.

COWBOY CAPITAL

Miles City is all about the Wild West! Ranchers come to town for the weekly livestock auction, while rodeo people from all over visit the annual Bucking Horse Sale.

DINOSAURS AND DIGS

Montana is one of the best places to find dinosaur fossils in the U.S. Ekalaka hosts the yearly Dino Shindig, with lectures from leading paleontologists, kids' activities, and live music.

LATINO HEROES

Latino people have been in Montana since before it was a state, first as fur traders, cowboys, and railroad workers. Today, many save lives as local community health workers.

JACK HORNER
B.1946
Paleontologist who discovered that some dinosaurs cared for their young. He was eight years old when he found his first bone.

JEANNETTE RANKIN
1880–1973
Born near Missoula, Rankin was the first woman elected to the U.S. Congress in 1916.

KEY FACTS

CAPITAL CITY
Helena

TOTAL POPULATION OF STATE
1,084,225

AREA OF STATE (SQ MI)
147,040

POPULATION OF CAPITAL
32,091

ASINIIWIN
1851/52–1916
An important Chippewa leader who was chief in Montana. He helped establish the Rocky Boy's Reservation.

Paleo-Indian peoples were the first to live in what is now Montana. Indigenous nations that have called the region home since then include the Blackfeet, Shoshone, Crow, Cheyenne, Kootenai, and the Salish. In the 1600s, the area became part of the French territory of Louisiana, and changed hands between France and Spain until the U.S. bought it in the Louisiana Purchase, in 1803. Amidst the arrival of the railroad and new European settlers, Montana was admitted as the 41st state in 1889.

Today, Montana is home to seven Indigenous reservations. It is the largest landlocked state in the mountainous west, known for wide-open spaces, grassy plains, and towering peaks. It's nicknamed the "Treasure State" for its booming history of mining and gold rushes. Montana is known for having the most mammal species of any state, the country's longest undammed river—Yellowstone—and Yogo sapphires, which are found only here and are considered to be one of the finest gemstones in the world. The state is sparsely populated but has its fair share of cowboys, rodeos, researchers, and miners!

Nebraska

The "Cornhusker State" is known for its vast plains, but Nebraska is anything but plain! The original home of Indigenous groups such as the Omaha and Pawnee, this area also boasts the historic Lewis and Clark expedition trail. When Nebraska became a state in 1867, European colonizers from Germany and Russia quickly staked their claim, turning the vast plains into farmland. The state is divided into two major land areas: the Great Plains, with its treeless prairies, and the Dissected Till Plains, with its rolling hills.

Today Nebraska is known for its historic expeditions and is home to a growing Latino population. Residents maintain the state's nickname by relying on corn as a major source of income, but the production of poultry and sheep is growing. Nebraska is a nature lover's paradise, with the world's largest forest planted by hand, over 80,000 miles of rivers, and the biggest mammoth skeleton ever found (nicknamed "Archie")! As a state famous for its pioneering spirit, Nebraskans continue to forge a new path to the future.

ZANZYE H. A. HILL
1906–1935
The first Black female law graduate from the University of Nebraska, she was also the first Black woman to practice law in the state.

JORGE GARCIA
B.1973
Best known for his role on the hit show *Lost*, Garcia is an actor and comedian from Omaha.

MALCOLM X
1925–1965
A civil rights leader and speaker, Malcolm was known for his strong opinions and activism.

ROXANE GAY
B.1974
Born in Omaha to Haitian parents, this passionate writer and professor is best known for her best-selling books.

FRANCIS LA FLESCHE
1857–1932
La Flesche was an Indigenous American who recorded the Omaha Indigenous culture and worked as a translator for the Smithsonian.

INDIGENOUS ARTIFACTS
The land now called Nebraska has a rich history of Indigenous American groups. The Stuhr Museum honors those groups, with its collection of Indigenous artifacts, such as pottery and clothing, dating back over 100 years.

GRAND ISLAND

KEARNEY

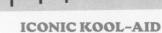

KEY FACTS

CAPITAL CITY
Lincoln

TOTAL POPULATION OF STATE
1,961,504

AREA OF STATE (SQ MI)
77,348

POPULATION OF CAPITAL
291,082

COW TOWN
Once known for its abundance of cows in the 19th century, Ogallala locals honor their past with a summer festival remembering the old cow days with food and fun!

WILD WILD WEST
Rodeos, Western wear, and a frontier-inspired musical are just a few things that you'll find at Nebraska's biggest state festival, NEBRASKAland Days!

ICONIC KOOL-AID
Known as Nebraska's favorite refreshment, this flavored drink mix was invented in Hastings and is now consumed the world over! Today, people can visit the popular Kool-Aid museum in Hastings.

LEWIS AND CLARK TRAIL

A HISTORIC JOURNEY
Spanning 4,900 miles between Pennsylvania and Oregon, the Lewis and Clark National Historic Trail is headquartered in Omaha. The trail connects 16 states and runs through tribal land. In the early 1800s, U.S. Army officers Meriwether Lewis and William Clark were asked to survey the land in the west as part of the Louisiana Purchase, to enable early settlers to learn more about the territory. Members of their party included a Shoshone woman named Sacagawea and an enslaved Black man named York. The trail has been visited by thousands. It is a symbol of hope and of the pioneer spirit.

CHICKEN EGGSTRAVAGANZA
Residents in Wayne host an annual chicken show complete with a Cluck-off, with locals competing for the title of best chicken "cluck" imitation.

HARVEST POWWOW
The historic Omaha Tribe hosts an annual harvest where visitors can learn more about the culture and watch dancing and singing contests.

STAR PARTY
Residents have fun exploring the stars at the annual Nebraska Star Party on a historic campsite. They even have a school where they teach newcomers how to stargaze!

HISPANIC HISTORIANS
With nearly 200,000 Hispanic Americans in the state, Nebraskans honor Latino and Hispanic culture with the El Museo Latino in Omaha. It provides education about the history and culture of the growing population.

GERMAN SOCIETY
With German ancestry representing about 43% of the state, the American Historical Society of Germans from Russia preserves German-Russian history in the area.

OMAHA

BELLEVUE

AFROMAHA
Omaha is home to the young Afromaha festival celebrating African culture. It's also home to the largest group of Sudanese refugees in the country.

NEBRASKA KNIGHTS
The Knights of Ak-Sar-Ben ("Nebraska" spelled in reverse) is a civic organization in Omaha that crowns a new Queen and King each summer in commemoration of the legendary search for the Golden Cities by Spanish explorer Francisco Vázquez de Coronado.

GPBHM
GREAT PLAINS BLACK HISTORY MUSEUM

LINCOLN

CZECH MATES
The annual Czech festival takes place in Wilbur, the nation's Czech capital! Residents celebrate their Czech roots by hosting a pageant and handmade quilt show.

QUILT QUIZZES
Residents in Lincoln boast an International Quilt Museum where locals and visitors can learn more about the tradition of quilting, as well as attend crafting workshops.

PLAINS BLACK CULTURE
Although Nebraska has fewer than 200,000 Black residents, Black culture is alive and well at the Great Plains Black History Museum, where achievements by local Black Americans are promoted and celebrated.

FUTURE FILMMAKERS
Voted as one of the top film festivals in the nation, the Omaha Film Festival showcases new talent and is known as one of the few film facilities for Omaha residents.

CAPITAL CITY
Carson City

TOTAL POPULATION OF STATE
3,104,614

AREA OF STATE (SQ MI)
110,572

POPULATION OF CAPITAL
58,639

FLOYD MAYWEATHER JR.
B. 1977
15-time world champion boxer who retired undefeated in 2017.

INDIGENOUS NEVADANS
The Great Basin Indigenous American tribes, the Washoe, Northern Paiute, Southern Paiute, and Western Shoshone, all call Nevada home. Their influence encouraged the state to replace Columbus Day with Indigenous Peoples' Day.

THE BURNING MAN FESTIVAL
One of the largest cultural events in the U.S. takes place in the Black Rock Desert. A symbolic ritual burning of a wooden effigy draws nearly 70,000 people to the big desert party celebrating self-expression.

THE BIGGEST LITTLE CITY IN THE WORLD

RENO

CARSON CITY

WHEAT FARMERS
Nevadans are known for their wheat. They grow more than $9.3 million worth of the crop every year.

ARTOWN
An annual month-long festival first started by local artists and businesspeople to save the declining town of Reno. Today, it attracts more than 300,000 people in celebration of all things artistic!

ASTRONAUT'S PLAYGROUND
The 400-acre Lunar Crater site in Nye County is the result of a volcanic explosion long ago. It was used as a training ground for NASA astronauts who were headed to the moon.

While no one is certain exactly when the first humans lived in present-day Nevada, rock carvings have been found that date back 14,800 years. In Hidden Cave, near the city of Fallon, there is evidence of human use 4,000–2,000 years ago. Nevada's contemporary Indigenous tribal nations include the Shoshone, Washoe, and Paiute. The land was claimed by Spanish colonists in 1519, and became a part of Mexico in 1821. In 1864, during the Civil War, the U.S. claimed Nevada as the 36th state.

Nevada is nicknamed the "Silver State" because of the large deposits of silver discovered here. It was part of the Wild West and home to the first railroad workers and ranchers. It has more mountain ranges than any other state, and its most famous city, Las Vegas, is the brightest place on Earth when viewed from outer space. Nevada was the first state to ratify the Fifteenth Amendment to the U.S. Constitution, which prohibits state and federal governments from denying a citizen's right to vote based on their "race, color, or previous condition of servitude." This allowed formerly enslaved people to vote for the first time.

ALIEN RESEARCHERS
Area 51, a U.S. Air Force military base and a nuclear test site, is believed by some to be an alien UFO research facility.

THE LOST CITY
The Lost City Museum preserves the remains of Indigenous cultures, which were submerged under Lake Mead when the Hoover Dam was built. Saved artifacts, many from the Pueblo Grande de Nevada site, date as far back as 8000 BCE.

NORTH LAS VEGAS
LAS VEGAS
PARADISE
HENDERSON

DAM CITY
The Hoover Dam is the single largest public works project in American history, with more than 3 million cubic yards of concrete. Not only did the project inspire the invention of hard hats, but the nearby Boulder City was created just to house the thousands of dam workers who built it.

MOBSTERS & SIN CITY
Las Vegas is now the "Entertainment Capital of the World," but it was once part of the Wild West. East Coast mobsters like Bugsy Siegel were drawn to the oasis and poured money into its development.

LAS VEGAS MELA

The Las Vegas Sikh community hosts the Vaisakhi Melas (Indian Food and Cultural Festival). The festival showcases the best of Indian culture, from jewelry to clothing and food to animated Bollywood dance routines. Sikh culture and religion is known to be very inclusive and has had a great influence over the food, dress, and traditions of Indians. The festival is a celebration of folk traditions and cultural heritage that focuses on the unique diversity of the city.

DIVERSITY MAGNET

Vegas has always drawn a diverse crowd with its abundance of service and construction jobs. It's now a mosaic of neighborhoods, including the Latino barrio in the northeast, a pan-Asian Chinatown in the west, and a Muslim community that includes Sub-Saharan Africans, Pakistanis, Arabs, and more.

SHRIMPERS

Las Vegans love shrimp, eating more than 60,000 pounds a day! They've even opened up one of the first desert shrimp farms, just to meet local demand.

HAWAIIAN NEVADANS

Las Vegas is called the "Ninth Island" because there are so many Hawaiians living there! The population of Hawaiians and other Pacific Islanders in the state has doubled in the past decade.

LOVEBIRDS

On average, 300 couples are married each day in Las Vegas. It's the top wedding destination in the country!

FEELING LUCKY!

Nevada has over 200,000 slot machines, one for every ten residents. The odds of winning big can be extremely low, but more than 41 million visitors still try their luck each year.

FORTUNE HUNTERS

Although nicknamed the "Silver State," Nevada is the largest gold-producing state in America and the fourth-largest in the world. Today, many still come to Nevada seeking riches, both underground and on gambling tables.

CARRIE DANN
1932–2021
Indigenous rancher and activist who, with her sister Mary, became famous for protesting the U.S. government's control of Indigenous land in Nevada.

RAFAEL RIVERA
C.1800
The 1829 Spanish explorer and scout for Mexican traders who gave the luscious green valley of Las Vegas its name, meaning "The Meadows."

JACOB DAVIS
1831–1908
Reno-based tailor credited for inventing blue jeans.

JENA MALONE
B.1984
Award-winning actress known for her role in *The Hunger Games*.

NEVADA

CANDY LOVERS
First opened in the 1880s, Chutters Candy Store in Littleton holds the Guinness World Record for the longest candy counter in the world. It is 112 feet long and still open to visiting sweet tooths!

THE ABENAKI AND PENNACOOK PEOPLE
In southern New Hampshire, there were once many groups of Algonquian-speaking peoples, living in many different tribes. Today, the Abenaki and Pennacook are the main two nations, living in Coos and Grafton.

PASSACONAWAY
1550/1570–1669
A 17th-century chief of the Pennacook people in what is now southern New Hampshire, who became "chief of chiefs" of a union of Indigenous groups in New England.

KEY FACTS

CAPITAL CITY
Concord

TOTAL POPULATION OF STATE
1,377,529

AREA OF STATE (SQ MI)
9,349

POPULATION OF CAPITAL
43,976

SKI JUMPERS
This is the only state that offers ski jumping as a high-school sport! Bode Miller—winner of six Olympics medals—learned the art of skiing in Franconia.

GAMERS' PARADISE
The American Classic Arcade Museum is the largest of its kind in the world! Its Annual Classic Video Game and Pinball Tournament has gamers from around the globe come and try to beat world-record high scores.

FEMALE TRAILBLAZERS
The first strike organized by female workers in America took place in Dover against the new policies that banned talking on the job.

we shall **FIGHT** until we **WIN!**

CRAFTY KNITTERS
Deerfield's Sheep and Wool Festival is a hub for knitters, felters, and sheep lovers. Attractions include herding dog demonstrations, spinning-technique workshops, and, of course, plenty of wool sales.

PORTSMOUTH BLACK HERITAGE TRAIL
A tour celebrates Black history with 40 sites that show how African Americans raised generations of family, built community, founded institutions, and served their town, state and nation.

PORTSMOUTH AFRICAN BURYING GROUND

Welcome to Manchester
The Queen City

MULTICULTURAL MANCHESTER
Full of international tastes, Queen City is a refugee resettlement area, home to ethnic groups from around the world. More than 80 languages are spoken at local schools.

MUSLIM GRASSROOTS
The Islamic Society of Greater Manchester is the largest mosque in the state. Amid protest, residents constructed it together. Local Bosnians did carpentry, one family provided carpeting, another the front door, and many volunteers helped to clear the wooded area where it was built.

ROCHESTER

CONCORD

DOVER

MANCHESTER

NASHUA

PARTY HOUSE
Madame Sherri's Castle in the forest of Chesterfield is a glamorous house where the eccentric costume designer threw decadent parties for New York's theater elite.

OUT-OF-THIS-WORLD PARTY
The famous 1965 sighting of strange sky lights in town inspired the now over-50-year-old Exeter UFO Festival.

SCOTTISH POTATOES
The first potato grown in the U.S. was planted in New Hampshire in 1719 by Scottish settlers. Today, it's New Hampshire's state vegetable.

FREE BOOKS!
The first free public library in America was established in 1833 in Peterborough.

INTERNATIONAL ARTISTS
The Andres Institute of Art and Sculpture Garden displays around 100 sculptures from artists all over the world. The art decorates Brookline's hiking trails surrounding this area.

MYSTERY HILL
In Salem, there is an archaeological structure dubbed "America's Stonehenge." It has been linked to various communities, including Irish monks, Indigenous Americans, British colonists, ancient Middle Eastern people, and 18th- and 19th-century farmers. No one knows for sure who built it or why.

New Hampshire

Humans have lived in what's now New Hampshire for at least 12,000 years. Thousands of years ago Indigenous peoples, including the Abenaki and the Pennacook, lived on the land. In the 1500s, the French and British empires arrived and fought over the territory. The British overcame the French, but New Hampshire became the epicenter for the American Revolution in 1776. It declared its independence from Great Britain and was named the ninth U.S. state in 1788.

New Hampshire has everything from mountain ranges and hilly valleys to coastlines and sandy beaches. The Granite State, as it is also known, is famous for more than just its granite quarries. It has the lowest poverty rate in the U.S. and is also one of the wealthiest in the Union. It is renowned for inventions like the snowmobile, its history as a center for the textile industry, tourism hotspots, apple cider doughnuts, and pickles.

ALAN BARTLETT SHEPARD JR
1923–1998
Born in Derry, he was the first American to travel into space.

RALPH HENRY BAER
1922–2014
Creator of the "Brown Box," a device that allowed players to control moving dots on a TV screen—the beginnings of the first ever video game.

SAGHIR "SAGGY" TAHIR
1944–2013
Believed to be the first Pakistani elected to a state legislature in the U.S. He was a member of the New Hampshire House of Representatives for four terms.

ADAM SANDLER
B.1966
American actor, comedian, screenwriter, and film producer who grew up in Manchester.

THE ANNUAL PICKLE FESTIVAL

The annual Pickle Festival in Winchester is an old-fashioned town fair, with live music, a parade, local craftsmen, and, of course, pickles. It began more than two decades ago in celebration of the town's Polish ancestry. Pickles are a staple of Polish cuisine. Alongside numerous pickle-themed floats, plenty of pickle costumes, and marching bands, are the main events: judging for the best jar of pickles and a pickle-eating contest!

FRIED PICKLES

SHAQUILLE O'NEAL
B.1972
Newark-born iconic basketball player and actor known for being a four-time NBA champion.

MUSICAL GENIUSES
An impressive musical legacy comes from this state. Bruce Springsteen, Frank Sinatra, Jon Bon Jovi, Whitney Houston, Lauryn Hill, and the Jonas Brothers and all hail from here!

LITTLE ISTANBUL
Paterson has the second-largest Muslim population in America. It has the largest Turkish American and second largest Arab American community in the country. Here signs in Turkish and Arabic welcome shoppers from everywhere.

PATERSON

NEWARK

JERSEY CITY

ELIZABETH

GARDEN STATE
Jersey folk have more than 10,000 farms and produce over 100 varieties of fruits and vegetables including squash, bell peppers, tomatoes, blueberries, peaches, and cranberries.

THE AFRICAN AMERICAN HERITAGE FESTIVAL
More than one million people come out to celebrate Newark's three-day African American Heritage Festival every year! The event includes parades, music, food, cultural stalls, seminars, , and skydivers who land in front of City Hall!

THE LATINO FESTIVAL
With growing communities of Puerto Ricans, Dominicans, and Mexicans, Monmouth County celebrates the diversity and contributions of Latin America in central Jersey every year.

QUEEN LATIFAH
B.1970
Newark-born pioneering rap artist who made a huge impact rapping about issues like women's empowerment and violence against Black women. She is also an award-winning actor and the first hip-hop artist with a star on Hollywood's walk of fame.

THE FIRST RESERVATION
Brotherton was the first Indigenous American reservation in the country, in 1758. The Lenape were forced there during the colonial period. Most tribes indigenous to New Jersey were forced to reservations in Oklahoma.

TRENTON

LAKEWOOD

IBTIHAJ MUHAMMAD
B.1985
Maplewood-native and Olympic fencing champion who became the first American athlete to compete in the Olympics in a hijab and the first Muslim American woman to win a medal in the Olympics.

ORATAM
C.1600
Sagamore, or chief, of the Hackensack, a subgroup of the Lenni-Lenape when the Dutch settlers arrived. He was known for his kind and diplomatic nature.

MASON DIXON LINE

THE CRADLE OF EMANCIPATION
With the help of the Quakers—the first organized group to speak against slavery—Burlington County became the largest community of free Black people in the state.

DINER CAPITAL OF THE WORLD
With more than 500, New Jersey is home to more diners than any other state! It's the perfect place for a quick bite for commuters between Philly and New York City.

JERSEY SMARTS
The state has more engineers and scientists per square mile than anywhere else in the world! It's known as the "Medicine Chest of the World" because of the many biotech and pharmaceutical companies based here.

GEORGE R. R. MARTIN
B.1948
Bayonne-born novelist, screenwriter, and television producer famous for his epic fantasy series *A Song of Ice and Fire*.

FREE HAVEN
Originally known as Free Haven, Lawnside borough was home to the first self-governing Black district in the North.

KITE RUNNERS
The world's largest kite festival is held yearly in Wildwood. Kite-makers from all over the world come to New Jersey to showcase their skills and talents in kite flying.

KEY FACTS

CAPITAL CITY
Trenton

TOTAL POPULATION OF STATE
9,288,994

AREA OF STATE (SQ MI)
8,723

POPULATION OF CAPITAL
90,871

INDIA SQUARE

Jersey City, also known as "Little India," celebrates its Indian American community with the Indian American festival, involving music, movies, and dance competitions.

HISPANIC NEW JERSEYANS

Many Hispanic and Latino communities live here. Union City is home to more Cubans than Havana, Cuba! Little Lima in Paterson is the largest Peruvian community outside of South America, and Ironbound is a Portuguese and Brazilian neighborhood in Newark.

CIAO, NEW JERSEY!

New Jersey's Italian community celebrates their ancestry with a four-day festival in Hoboken, which includes an 800-pound Madonna sculpture, pizza- and cannoli-eating contests, musical performances, and a grape-stomping competition!

JERSEY JOKERS

Jersey is the birthplace of countless funny people, including Chelsea Handler and Danny DeVito!

Indigenous peoples first lived in New Jersey about 15,000 years ago. They included the Lenni-Lenape, a tribe that formed part of the Algonquin nation. Around 1524 the Italian explorer Giovanni da Verrazzano visited, followed by Swedish, Finnish, and Dutch colonists. They fought over the land until the British Empire claimed New Jersey as a colony. In 1787, it officially became the third state to join the Union.

New Jersey is approximately halfway between the equator and North Pole, giving it five unique climates that make it ideal for many crops. Hence the state's nickname, "the Garden State." It has the first, busiest, and most complex transportation systems in the world. It was also the first state to sign the Bill of Rights, the first to host an organized and a professional basketball game, the first to have a boardwalk, and the first town wired for electricity.

New Jersey

KOREATOWN AND CHUSEOK

Bergen County has the highest density of Koreans in the Western Hemisphere. Broad Avenue is called a "Korean food walk of fame" and Palisades Park has the most Korean restaurants within a one-mile radius in America. The colorful Koreatown community shares their annual tradition of celebrating Chuseok, the harvest moon festival, with other Jersey folk. Every year tens of thousands of people come out to enjoy traditional Korean food, including the holiday's central dish, songpyeon, a Korean rice cake, and to enjoy music including Korean folk, rock, and K-pop!

NEW MEXICO

TRAIN BUFFS
The Cumbres & Toltec trainline, originally built to serve miners, has been featured in more than 20 movies, such as *Indiana Jones and the Last Crusade*, and is now a popular destination for train enthusiasts.

NUCLEAR SCIENTISTS
Los Alamos National Laboratory started up in 1943. The lab had a single purpose: build an atomic bomb. Scientists here still research nuclear technology and other subjects related to national security and energy.

AMERICAN WEST HOSPITALITY
19th-century traders, settlers, and outlaws journeyed from Missouri to Santa Fe on the Santa Fe Trail. In Cimarron's Express St. James Hotel, established in 1872, there are bullet holes in the ceiling from real bar fights!

NAVAJO NATION
In the northeast of the Navajo Nation, which spans three states, Shiprock towers over the desert. This natural formation is sacred to the Navajo, and is known as Tsé Bit' a'i, or "rock with wings."

ANCESTRAL PUEBLOANS
Between 900 and 1150 CE, Ancestral Puebloans built huge stone palaces in what is now the Chaco Culture National Historical Park. Many of these impressive buildings have mysterious alignments with the sun and stars.

ANCIENT GRAFFITI
At El Morro National Monument, over 2,000 signatures and messages dot the rock. Discover who passed through before you, from Ancestral Puebloans to Spanish missionaries and 19th-century U.S. soldiers.

STAR GAZERS
The Gila National Forest was the continent's first dark-sky sanctuary. Amateur astronomers visit on dark, clear nights to drink in the amazing white ribbon of the Milky Way.

HISPANIC HERITAGE
Visit the National Hispanic Cultural Center in Albuquerque to experience Hispanic dance, art, poetry, and more.

MOGOLLON CULTURE
Nomadic people sheltered in caves next to the Gila River for thousands of years. In the late 1200s, the people of the Mogollon culture built sturdy stone homes in the cliff side. You can still explore them today.

SANTA FE

RIO RANCHO

ALBUQUERQUE

SPACE TOURISTS
Spaceport America is the world's first airport built specifically for commercial space travel. The first commercial space flight has yet to take off, but engineers are already testing designs at the spaceport.

ROSWELL

LAS CRUCES

CHILI FARMERS
Hatch, New Mexico, is known as the chili capital of the world. Farmers have been growing these tasty, spicy peppers for many generations. One green chili pod has the same amount of vitamin C as six oranges!

GEM HUNTERS
Rockhound State Park in the Little Florida Mountains is a magnet for gem and mineral hunters. Search for geodes, jasper, onyx, obsidian, and quartz crystals. Amateur collectors are even allowed to take some home!

UFO HUNTERS
In July 1947, a rancher near Roswell discovered some strange metal wreckage. Many UFO enthusiasts believe it was the remains of a flying saucer piloted by aliens! Roswell has a museum dedicated to the mysterious and unexplained incident.

KEY FACTS

CAPITAL CITY
Santa Fe

TOTAL POPULATION OF STATE
2,117,522

AREA OF STATE (SQ MI)
121,590

POPULATION OF CAPITAL
87,505

NEW MEXICO'S CUISINE

New Mexico's cuisine is truly special! A unique fusion of Puebloan Indigenous American and Hispanic food culture, red and green chilies feature highly. Favorite dishes include green chili stew, biscochitos, and natillas.

TLAXCALA TRADITION

Sometime between 1610 and 1626, Tlaxcalan people built the Church of San Miguel in Santa Fe. The church has been rebuilt many times, but parts of the original structure survive, making it the oldest church in the continental U.S.

AMAZING ARTISTS

Founded in 1610, Santa Fe is the oldest capital city in North America. Now it's known as a creative hub. Artists of all ages make everything from paintings and giant outdoor murals to textile sculptures and installations.

MABEL DODGE LUHAN
1879–1962
A writer and patron of the arts, Luhan hosted some of the most famous artists of the early 20th century at her Taos home.

POPÉ
C.1630–C.1692
A Tewa leader who headed the Pueblo Revolt in 1680 against Spanish colonists. He drove them out of Santa Fe temporarily and reestablished a traditional way of life for Indigenous people.

ANNIE DODGE WAUNEKA
1910–1997
A public health champion for the Navajo Nation, offering radio broadcasts and creating an English-Navajo medical dictionary. She was also one of the first women elected to the Tribal Council.

MICHAEL REYNOLDS
B.1945
An architect who uses recycled materials like old tires and glass bottles. He has designed off-the-grid homes, called Earthships, that store the warmth of the sun and don't require any fossil fuels to heat. You can see a community of them near Taos.

MARIE Z. CHINO
1907–1982
A famous ceramist, who inspired a movement to use ancient Mimbres designs on modern pottery. She was born at Acoma Pueblo—the oldest continuously inhabited settlement in North America.

For at least 12,000 years, human beings have roamed the desert, canyons, and high snowy peaks of what is currently known as New Mexico. Today, there are 19 Indigenous American pueblos in the state as well as the Navajo Nation and three Apache tribes. Spanish imperialists first arrived in the mid-1500s looking for mythical cities full of treasure. In the late 16th century they claimed the land, even though it was already inhabited. You can still explore their churches and palaces. In 1850, New Mexico became a U.S. territory, but it didn't become a state until 1912.

Today English, Spanish, and Navajo are the three most spoken languages in the state. In Navajo, "yá'át'ééh" is a friendly greeting that loosely translates to "all is well." This state attracts all sorts of people, from artists and healers to outdoor enthusiasts and green chile lovers. With plenty of sunshine, big blue skies, and clear starry nights, New Mexico is known as the land of enchantment.

NEW YORK

JAY-Z
B.1969
Brooklyn-born rapper crowned hip-hop's first billionaire and regarded as one of the most influential hip-hop artists in history.

JOHN BROWN
1800–1859
Abolitionist who organized a rebellion against slave owners at Harpers Ferry, West Virginia. Brown is buried in New York.

ALEXANDRIA OCASIO-CORTEZ
B.1989
Bronx-born Puerto Rican American who is the youngest woman to ever take office in U.S. Congress, at just 29 years old.

YASIIN BEY
B.1973
Iconic rapper, singer, songwriter, and actor turned activist from Brooklyn, better known as Mos Def.

LADY GAGA
B.1986
One of the best-selling music artists of all time born and raised in NYC.

NY MUSLIMS
In the 1980s, a neighborhood in Tompkins was settled by mainly Black Muslims seeking to escape the troubles and overcrowding of NYC. Despite being targeted by white extremists, Islamberg has maintained a reputation of friendliness and charity.

ROCHESTER

SYRACUSE

HAUDENOSAUNEE LEGACY
First established in the 17th century, the Ganondagan State Historic Site is a Seneca village and protected landmark.

BUFFALO

NATIONAL WOMEN'S HALL OF FAME
Est. 1969

LEADING WOMEN
The National Women's Hall of Fame in Seneca Falls celebrates iconic American women, such as Ruth Bader Ginsburg, Sojourner Truth, Sacagawea, and Oprah Winfrey.

ALBANY

ALBANIAN NEW YORKERS
Albanians first immigrated to America in the 1880s. Today, the Bronx is home to the largest community of Albanians in the country.

SPANISH HARLEM
East Harlem is home to one of the biggest Hispanic communities in the state. It's mostly made up of Puerto Ricans, Cubans, Mexicans, and the largest Dominican population in the country, and is known for its Latin freestyle and salsa music.

YONKERS

NEW YORK

BLACK NEW YORK
NYC has the largest Black community of any American city! The city has birthed countless icons including 50 Cent, Ashanti, Alicia Keys, Eddie Murphy, Michael Jordan, and Denzel Washington, among others.

APOLLO
AMATEUR NIGHT

CHINESE AMERICANS
NYC has at least nine Chinatowns. The most famous is Manhattan's, in one of the city's first immigrant neighborhoods.

AMATEUR MUSICIANS
The Apollo was the first theater in the U.S. to allow Black people to perform. Greats such as Aretha Franklin and Ella Fitzgerald have graced the boards. Today, hopefuls perform at the legendary amateur night.

ITALIAN NEW YORK
The state's largest European ethnic community is the Italian Americans. While Manhattan's Little Italy district used to have the largest Italian community, today Staten Island claims the title.

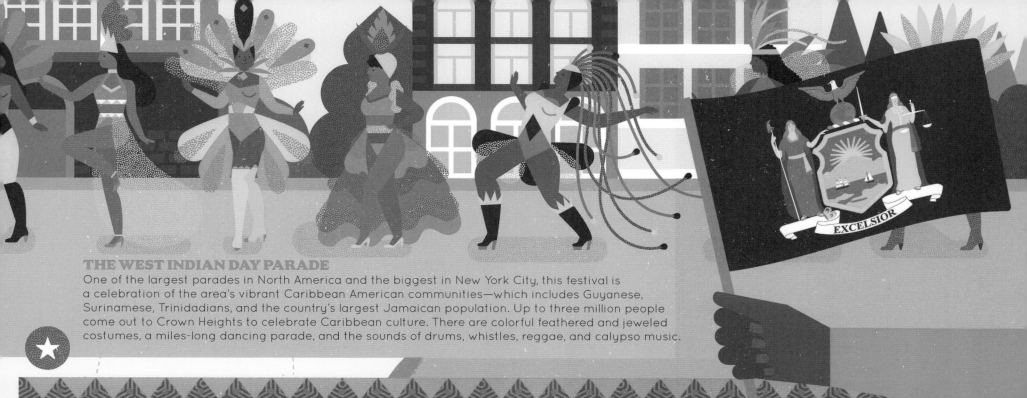

THE WEST INDIAN DAY PARADE

One of the largest parades in North America and the biggest in New York City, this festival is a celebration of the area's vibrant Caribbean American communities—which includes Guyanese, Surinamese, Trinidadians, and the country's largest Jamaican population. Up to three million people come out to Crown Heights to celebrate Caribbean culture. There are colorful feathered and jeweled costumes, a miles-long dancing parade, and the sounds of drums, whistles, reggae, and calypso music.

Over 5,000 years ago, New York was home to many Indigenous groups. In the 1100s, their descendants formed the Haudenosaunee Confederacy, an alliance that is today recognized as one of the world's oldest democracies. The Dutch arrived in New York in the 1600s and claimed the land, taking it from the local Indigenous population. When the British invaded in 1664, they claimed New York as a colony. In 1788, after the American Revolution, New York officially became the 11th state of America.

Today, the Empire State, nicknamed for its strategic location on the Atlantic Ocean, is home to people from all over the globe. It is a place filled with great natural beauty, from the snowy peaks of the Adirondack and Catskill Mountains to the magnificent Niagara Falls. It is also home to what many consider the cultural capital of the world: New York City. NYC is the most populous and diverse city in the country, where nearly 800 languages are spoken. Its immigrant population chiefly come from the Dominican Republic, China, Jamaica, Russia, Italy, Poland, and India. It is the birthplace of many movements that have changed the course of human history and changed the worlds of music, art, fashion, film, and finance.

ARAB TOWNS
Arab American enclaves have formed throughout NYC and include Little Yemen, Little Syria, and Little Egypt, but residents of these neighborhoods hail from more than 20 countries!

INDIGENOUS NY
Queens hosts the Annual Thunderbird American Indian Powwow, NYC's largest and oldest powwow, or gathering, of Indigenous peoples. Every July, over 40 nations celebrate Indigenous American heritage.

HASIDIC JEWS
Williamsburg is home to one of the largest Hasidic communities in the world, which includes many Holocaust survivors. NYC itself has a larger Jewish population than any other city in the world!

IRISH HERITAGE
With a chorus of bagpipes and nearly two million spectators, NYC's St. Patrick's Day Parade is the world's largest and oldest Irish parade. It's been running since 1762 after the first Irish immigrants came to North America.

LITTLE RUSSIA
The largest Russian-speaking community in America lives on Brighton Beach. The annual Brighton Jubilee celebrates the neighborhood's Russian heritage.

JACKSON HEIGHTS SPLIT
This Queens neighborhood is one of the most diverse in the state. It is home to two-thirds of all Bangladeshi Americans and the largest Pakistani American community in the country, as well as large populations of Colombians, Ecuadorians, Argentinians, Indians, and Nepalese.

KEY FACTS

CAPITAL CITY
Albany

TOTAL POPULATION OF STATE
20,201,249

AREA OF STATE (SQ MI)
54,555

POPULATION OF CAPITAL
99,224

From the Appalachian Mountains to sandy coastal beaches and historic landmarks, North Carolina is a Southern jewel. In 1789 it became a state. The area was inhabited by the Chowanoke before European colonizers arrived, making it one of the first 13 colonies. Soon, the state began to prosper off the back of enslaved laborers forced to work on tobacco farms. By the 21st century, North Carolina had been through many changes: from a Confederate state, to the site of the world's first airplane flight, to a tourist hotspot treasured for its natural beauty.

Today, North Carolina is a diverse area known for its vineyards, barbecue, strawberries, and blueberries. The state is also dedicated to improving the way we use energy by utilizing hydroelectric power and encouraging careers in STEM (science, technology, engineering, math). While maintaining some of the charm and industry of past years, North Carolina is a state that upholds its traditions while looking to future progress.

THE FOUNTAIN OF YOUTH
Scientists at the Duke Lemur Center in Durham study lemurs and bush babies, because of their sleep patterns, to try to uncover the secrets of living longer.

THE RESEARCH TRIANGLE PARK HEADQUARTERS

THE TRIANGLE
The Triangle gets its name from the Research Triangle Park, which encompasses three research universities just minutes apart from each other. These centers provide hundreds of jobs for locals.

FREEDOM HILL
Incorporated in 1885 by freed people, the area once known as Freedom Hill is the oldest town founded by African Americans in the state. Today it is called Princeville and is home to over 2,000 people.

FREEDOM HILL

FURNITURE CAPITAL
High Point is known as the "Furniture Capital of the World" and is home to the world's largest furniture store. Over 200,000 people visit the area annually.

GREENSBORO

DURHAM

ASHE COUNTY CHRISTMAS
When it comes to Christmas trees, Ashe County is one of the top producers in the state! Some 13,000 growers boast an estimated 40,000 acres of trees.

WINSTON-SALEM

RALEIGH

FINGER-PICKING BLUES
This style of blues was made popular by musicians in the northern part of the state. The guitarist picks their fingers across the guitar strings in a style called Piedmont blues.

SWEET POTATO LAND
North Carolina farmers produce the highest number of sweet potatoes in the nation! Over 700 million pounds of the yummy potatoes are produced yearly.

BLUE MOUNTAIN DRIVE
Motorcyclists and bicyclists love driving down the 469-mile Blue Ridge Parkway. With scenic views of mountains, no wonder the route is known as "America's favorite drive!"

ASHEVILLE

CHARLOTTE

POTTERS PARADISE
Half of the population in Seagrove, North Carolina, are potters! Nicknamed the "Handmade Pottery Capital of the U.S.," there are more than 70 studios in the area, regular festivals, and unique pottery for all to enjoy.

FARMER'S BALL
Traditional Appalachian dances like the Shoo-Fly Swing are kept alive at this weekly contest in Swannanoa, near Asheville.

JAM SESSION
Asheville locals flock to the Pritchard Park Drum Circle for a weekly jam session where dozens of drummers play for fun.

BLACK HISTORY GARDEN
The Burton Street Community Peace Gardens in Asheville are filled with colorful art that pay homage to inspiring figures in Black History.

LORETTA LYNCH
B.1959
Lynch is the first African American woman to serve as the attorney general for the United States.

PACHINKO PARLOR
A Japanese-style pinball game, pachinko is a popular activity in Wilmington. Here residents can play at the only American parlor dedicated to the game.

CHEROKEE THEATER

The town of Cherokee in the Great Smoky Mountains is the traditional home of the Eastern Band of Cherokee Indians. The group keeps its history alive by hosting a summer production about the Trail of Tears, when over 16,000 Cherokees were forced out of their homes and onto a path to the west. The play is called *Unto These Hills* and shows every night from June through August. It's a drama that includes traditional music and dance. Visitors can also learn more about Indigenous American history at the nearby Cherokee Museum.

WATCHING WILD HORSES

Residents of Corolla enjoy watching wild horses roam free on the area's Currituck Banks.

DRAGON BOAT CLUB

Stemming from Chinese tradition, boaters in Raleigh gather to paddle dragon boats, long vessels that hold 20 paddlers. It is one of the fastest-growing aquatic sports in the world.

KEY FACTS

CAPITAL CITY
Raleigh

TOTAL POPULATION OF STATE
10,439,388

AREA OF STATE (SQ MI)
53,819

POPULATION OF CAPITAL
467,665

MAY 20th 1775

N★C

APRIL 12th 1776

SHIRLEY CAESAR
B.1938
Known as the "Queen of Gospel Music," Caesar is an award-winning singer and pastor.

KIZZMEKIA CORBETT
B.1986
Noted as one of the future leaders of the study of diseases, Corbett worked to understand and develop a vaccine for COVID-19.

RICKY HURTADO
B.1988
The first Latino Democrat elected to North Carolina's House of Representatives. He was sworn in in January 2021.

JULIANNE MOORE
B.1960
Moore is an award-winning actor and author known for her popular roles in films like *The Hunger Games.*

NORTH CAROLINA

MUSLIM ROOTS
A small Muslim community still gathers in Ross to practice at the historic site of the oldest still-standing mosque in the U.S.

VIKING HERITAGE
Many North Dakotans acknowledge their Scandinavian roots by celebrating with the annual Norsk festival. Attendees eat food like Norwegian waffles and Swedish meatballs, sell crafts, and share the culture.

SWING YOUR PARTNER!
Folks in North Dakota love to square dance so much it became the state's official American folk dance.

PASTA PARTY
Grand Forks residents hold a huge party each year to celebrate pasta! Most of the pasta in the nation comes from North Dakota.

BEEF BUFFS
Ranchers in this state make enough beef for 113 million hamburgers each year! There are more cattle than people in North Dakota.

MINOT

UKRAINIAN CULTURE
In Dickinson, the Ukrainian Cultural Institute works to preserve the rich history of Ukrainian North Dakotans.

COOL CAR COLLECTORS
Residents of Mandan love their classic cars, and what better way to celebrate than to host an annual event showcasing older-model cars cruising down Main Street?

CHURCH GROUPS
North Dakota has thousands of Christian churchgoers. The state boasts more churches per capita than any other.

GRAND FORKS

WEST FARGO

FARGO

BISMARCK

LESLIE BIBB
B.1974
This actor has been in numerous films, including Marvel's *Iron Man*!

SUNFLOWER POWER
With so much land in the state, it's no wonder that residents planted big sunflowers to beautify the area! North Dakota is the state that grows the most sunflowers in the nation.

YOUTH POWWOW
The Indigenous American youth of Bismarck participate in the annual International Powwow, where dancers and singers compete.

PEGGY LEE
1920–2002
A composer and songwriter, Lee was a popular singer whose career spanned seven decades.

KEY FACTS

CAPITAL CITY
Bismarck

TOTAL POPULATION OF STATE
779,094

AREA OF STATE (SQ MI)
70,698

POPULATION OF CAPITAL
73,622

Named for the Sioux people who first lived in the area, North Dakota is known for its snowy months and sunny flowers. Before European settlers arrived, the land known as North Dakota belonged to the Lakota and Dakota Sioux peoples, who continue to make up a significant portion of the population today. In 1889, North Dakota became a state and new settlers, such as Norwegians, moved into the area. The population continued to grow into the 20th century. Agriculture was king until the state saw the rise of oil exploration. The oil industry created a new economy in the sparsely populated state.

Today, North Dakota is still one of the least populated states, where snow falls every month except July and August! The state's farmland and ranches help sustain the nation in soybean and canola production. Populations of iconic bison, or buffalo, roam the grassy prairie. The state boasts a strong economy with its natural resources and agriculture, alongside its breathtaking natural landscapes.

NORTH DAKOTA

JOSH DUHAMEL
B.1972
An actor and model, Duhamel is best known for his role in the *Transformers* films.

PANCAKE RACE
There's nothing like a Midwestern pancake! In 2008, Fargo residents hosted the largest pancake event in the world, feeding 38,000 pancake lovers.

OH, HONEY, HONEY!
With over 530,000 honey bee colonies in the state, North Dakotans produce the most honey in the nation.

THE BIG ONE!
Residents of Fargo attend the Annual Fargo Fall Show. With over 300 booths from local crafters and artists, it's no wonder the community calls it "The Big One!"

MIDWEST KIDS
Fargo's Island Park is home to a colorful, fun-filled annual celebration for North Dakota's children. Families can enjoy local food and petting zoos here.

COUNTING SHEEP
North Dakota has the largest sheep research center in the nation, also used as a teaching facility. Students learn flock management, how to properly shear sheep, and even how to grade wool.

JAMES BUCHLI
B.1945
A retired U.S. Marine and astronaut, Buchli flew four space-shuttle missions.

JAMES ROSENQUIST
1933–2017
Rosenquist is famous for his pop art paintings that feature both iconic and everyday objects like drink bottles and kitchen appliances!

GOOD PLAIN ART
Residents of Fargo enjoy a fine arts scene that is housed in the city's downtown museum. The museum has 3,000 works including regional and Indigenous American art. It also hosts renowned national artists like Andy Warhol. At one time, this popular museum even went mobile—by sharing its collection across North Dakota in a semi-trailer! The Great Plains may be packed with farmland, ranches, and sunflowers, but residents always leave room to appreciate art.

PLAINS ART MUSEUM

# Ohio

DEHART HUBBARD
1903–1976
First African American athlete to win a gold medal in an individual event at the Olympics. In 1924, in Paris, he won the gold medal for the long jump.

TOLEDO

CLEVELAND

AKRON

TWIN DAYS
DOUBLE TAKE PARADE

MEDICAL MYSTERIES
The "Things Swallowed" display at the Allen County Museum showcases items that patients digested and which were retrieved by doctors! It includes buttons, thumbtacks, bones, coins, dentures, and lots more.

GROOVY GLACIER
Glacial Grooves State Memorial on Kelleys Island preserves the patterns carved into bedrock by a huge ice sheet 18,000 years ago.

RUBBER MAKERS
Akron is the rubber capital of the world. It used to produce over one third of all tires in the country.

DOUBLE TAKE
The world's largest annual gathering of twins, Twins Days, is held in Twinsburg where every pair dresses the same for the day!

EMERGENCY CALLS
The state has the world's oldest manufacturer of ambulances. It is also where the first known hospital-based ambulance service was based.

GREENHOUSE EXPERTS
Ohio is the leading producer of greenhouse and nursery plants. They grow crops floating in nutrient-rich water and soil-less containers.

AMISH COUNTRY
This is one of the largest Amish communities in the nation. They're known for their plain attire, simple lifestyles, and masterful handicrafts.

A STICKY SITUATION
For years, Maid-Rite Sandwich Shop's customers have been sticking their gum on the walls outside. Three of the building's four walls are covered in gum!

NEWCOMER HUB
Columbus welcomes refugees, immigrants, and new Americans. It is a hub for new Muslim Americans who have been central to Ohio's economic growth.

COLUMBUS

THE BEST CHEESE IN AMERICA
Agriculture is the state's largest industry. Its cheesemakers have helped the state rank number one in Swiss cheese production.

BIRTH OF BASEBALL
The Cincinnati Red Stockings, founded in 1869, were the first professional baseball team.

INTERFAITH WALK OF PEACE
CITY OF SPRINGFIELD

ISLAMIC DAY IN OHIO
The Islamic Council of Ohio hosts Islamic Day to help people better understand Islam and the growing Muslim community. The day is filled with interfaith events and activities, like a cultural fair.

NEWARK EARTHWORKS
The Newark Earthworks are ancient structures made from earth piled in geometric patterns. They are wonders left by the Hopewell culture, which flourished from 100 BCE to 500 CE.

CINCINNATI

SERPENT MOUND
This large earthen sculpture of a coiling serpent was built around 1000 CE, but historians don't know for certain who made it. It may have been either the Adena or Fort Ancient cultures.

TECUMSEH
1768–1813
Shawnee chief and resistance leader who fought to prevent the U.S. settling Indigenous lands.

U.S. PRESIDENTS
Seven American presidents were born in Ohio! It's filled with historical spots where the presidents lived and are remembered.

Paleo-Indian nomads first arrived in Ohio at the end of the Ice Age, where they hunted and gathered. Thousands of years later, Indigenous American tribal nations including the Erie, Kickapoo, and Shawnee lived on the land. The first Europeans arrived in the 1600s, beginning with French explorer René-Robert Cavelier, Sieur de La Salle. More followed, drawn by the booming fur trade. In 1763, the British claimed the land and Ohio became the 17th state in 1803.

Ohio is a Midwestern state in the Great Lakes region. Its name comes from the Haudenosaunee word "ohi-yo," meaning "great river." Ohio's landscape ranges from vast plains to the Appalachian Plateau, a region of steep cliffs and deep valleys. Its capital, Columbus, is a bustling metropolis, but the state is also known for its varied farmland. The Buckeye State—named after its famous buckeye tree—is known for many things, including inventing the hard candy, Life Savers, having the first concrete streets, and the Rock and Roll Hall of Fame.

KEY FACTS

CAPITAL CITY
Columbus

TOTAL POPULATION OF STATE
11,799,448

AREA OF STATE (SQ MI)
44,826

POPULATION OF CAPITAL
905,748

NEIL ARMSTRONG
1930–2012
The first person to walk on the Moon was born in Wapakoneta.

STEVEN SPIELBERG
B.1946
Award-winning film director behind blockbusters like *Ready Player One*, *Jaws*, and *Jurassic Park*.

ASA LONG
1904–1999
A checkers player who holds Guinness World Records as both the youngest and oldest national champion.

CLEVELAND GARLIC FESTIVAL
Dubbed the "smelliest in the state," this festival showcases over 300 garlic varieties. The event has garlic-inspired food, competitions, and live entertainment, including a Garlic Grill-Off where chefs compete to create unique dishes with garlic.

WHERE THE BUFFALO ROAM

It's estimated that over 30 million American bison, also called buffalo, roamed North America nearly two centuries ago. By the early 20th century, that number was down to 1,000. Thankfully, President Theodore Roosevelt and other conservationists made efforts to protect the bison from extinction. They established the American Bison Society at the Bronx Zoo in New York. 15 bison left the zoo, heading out for the great plains and mountains of Oklahoma. Today, there are 650 American bison descended from that early group. They roam freely over 59,000 acres at the Wichita Mountains Wildlife Refuge near Lawton.

HISPANIC HERITAGE

The town of Guymon was nearly deserted until Hispanic citizens and immigrants moved into the now bustling area, in the late 1960s.

COW CHIPPERS

The annual World Cow Chip Throwing Contest is held in Beaver. Locals line up to see who can toss the "chips" of dried cow poop the furthest!

COWBOYS OF THE PAST

Oklahoma City is home to the National Cowboy and Western Heritage Museum, where visitors can view the largest collection of bronco-busting exhibits.

KIOWA TRIBE

The bison-hunting Kiowa Tribe is known for its fierce resistance to U.S. expansion into its territory. They were forcibly resettled in Oklahoma in 1868.

FORT SILL APACHES

This tribe is most famous for their fearless leader Geronimo, who fought against the settlers in hopes of freedom for his people. The community still holds on to their traditions.

 LAWTON

During the early 1800s, Oklahoma was designated an "Indian Territory," and many Indigenous Americans were forcibly relocated here. As they began to to turn their new land into a home, ranchers and other settlers came to the state. These groups were nicknamed "Sooners" because they rushed to the land before President Harrison officially opened it for settlement. The Indigenous population, who had been promised their own nation, established the Sequoyah state in 1905. Two years later, Sequoyah combined with the Oklahoma Territory to officially become the 46th state.

With historic mountain ranges, mesas, and great plains, Oklahoma's natural beauty is reminiscent of the Old West. The state is also a major natural gas and oil producer. Today, there are 39 recognized Indigenous American tribal nations in Oklahoma, who have fought to keep their traditions alive. Oklahoma boasts a diverse population, a powerful history, and a strong connection to its cultural heritage.

LENA BLACKBIRD
1933–2021

Best known for her Cherokee double-walled basket weaving, Blackbird's popular basket patterns have earned her the title "National Living Treasure."

CADDO CERAMICS

Indigenous artists with Red River Valley roots keep their heritage alive through their popular pottery.

OKLAHOMA

CINEPHILES
Cinema buffs can still catch a silent film with a working pipe organ, just like in the 1920s, at Coleman Theater in Miami.

QUAPAW CUISINE
The historic Quapaw Nation supplies the meat and produce from their own cattle to the Red Oak Steakhouse.

HODA KOTB
B.1964
Born to Egyptian immigrants in Norman, Kotb is a journalist and the co-host of a popular national morning show.

RALPH ELLISON
1914–1994
Novelist who wrote *Invisible Man*, considered one of the great novels of American literature.

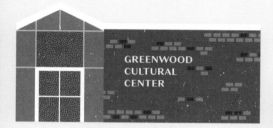

GREENWOOD DISTRICT
Once an area for African Americans during segregation, this district was destroyed in the 1921 Tulsa race riot. Today, residents can learn about Tulsa's history at the Greenwood Cultural Center.

SECRET CIRCUS
An empty wooded lot near Oklahoma City hosts an abandoned circus camp known as Gandini's Circus.

CHEROKEE NATION
As the largest Indigenous nation in the U.S., the Cherokee are widely known for their beadwork and carved pipes.

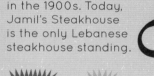

✳ **TULSA**
✳ **BROKEN ARROW**

LEBANESE CULTURE
Lebanese immigrants settled in the Tulsa area in the 1900s. Today, Jamil's Steakhouse is the only Lebanese steakhouse standing.

Jamil's

OKLAHOMA CITY
NORMAN

ROSY ROCKS
You'll find a collection of crystals shaped like roses at the Timberlake Rose Rock Museum in Noble.

VIETNAMESE HOTSPOT
Vietnamese immigrants arrived in Oklahoma City in the 1970s. Since then, their food has become some of the most popular cuisine in the area.

FOSSIL FIND
Fossil finders flock to Norman's Sam Noble Oklahoma Museum of Natural History to see the largest land-animal skull ever found: that of a pentaceratops that lived around 70 million years ago.

KEY FACTS

CAPITAL CITY
Oklahoma City

TOTAL POPULATION OF STATE
3,959,353

AREA OF STATE (SQ MI)
69,899

POPULATION OF CAPITAL
681,054

MATT KEMP
B.1984
Award-winning professional baseball outfielder who hails from Midwest City.

MYRA YVONNE CHOUTEAU
1929–2016
Celebrated dancer who was the youngest ballerina admitted to the prestigious Ballet Russe de Monte Carlo school. Established the first ballet school in Oklahoma.

OREGONIAN CHEESE
The Tillamook Cheese Factory is one of the largest cheese factories in the country! Local cheesemakers produce 171,000 pounds of cheese each day.

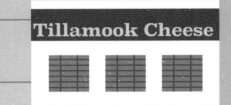

TREASURE HUNTING
Local legend has it that there's buried pirate treasure somewhere on Neahkahnie Mountain. The story has been passed down for generations, and inspired hoards of treasure hunters!

KEY FACTS

CAPITAL CITY
Salem

TOTAL POPULATION OF STATE
4,237,256

AREA OF STATE (SQ MI)
98,379

POPULATION OF CAPITAL
175,535

GREEN – LIVING LOVERS
In 1971 Oregon became the first state to ban the use of non-returnable bottles and cans. As a result, they reduced 40% of roadside litter!

WORLD BEAT FESTIVAL
Salem's big World Beat Festival highlights music, dance and food from over 70 cultures and nations, with the goal of establishing the city as a culturally rich and welcoming place.

GRAPE GROWERS
There are more than 900 vineyards in Oregon. Winemakers produce over 100 different varieties of grapes to make wine.

THE CONFEDERATED TRIBES OF GRAND RONDE
Over 30 different tribes and bands removed by the U.S. government now live on this reservation community. Despite a history of erasure, the community continues to thrive.

HILLSBORO GRESHAM

PORTLAND

THE CONFEDERATED TRIBES OF GRAND RONDE

SALEM

EUGENE

LATINO OREGONIANS
Oregon's Latino community is growing. They have deep roots beginning early in the 1800s, when Mexicans mined gold and tended livestock as *vaqueros*, or cowboys.

MUSHROOM HUNTERS
Hunting for rare mushrooms is a popular pastime for Oregonians who host an annual festival, the Estacada Festival of the Fungus.

REBELS
Southern Oregonians have been trying to secede from the Union since 1941. Disgruntled with a lack of representation, they renamed the area the "State of Jefferson." Every Thursday Jeffersonians stop highway traffic to announce their intentions.

THE GREAT SEAL OF STATE OF JEFFERSON

Evidence of humans in present-day Oregon dates back almost 15,000 years, making them some of the earliest to live in North America. Researchers also found the oldest shoes in the world when they discovered 70 pairs of sandals dating back ten millennia in an Oregon cave! In later centuries, Indigenous groups including the Paiute, Nez Perce, Shasta, Tillamook, Chinook, and many more lived on the land. Europeans arrived in the 1500s, including settlers from Spain and England, who tried claiming the land for themselves. In 1803 the Americans bought the land as part of the Louisiana Purchase. American settlers wheeled in by the wagonload using the westbound route, the Oregon Trail. In 1859, Oregon became the 33rd state.

Oregon is known as the "Beaver State," because of its history as a destination for fur-trappers. This Pacific Northwestern region is famous for a few things, including its record-breaking geography. It has the deepest lake in America, Crater Lake, the deepest river gorge on the continent, Hells Canyon, and the most deserted locations in the country, called ghost towns. Oregonians have a special love for roses, hazelnuts, mountain climbing, and shrubbery!

TY BURRELL
B.1967
Award-winning actor and comedian who started acting in the small town of Grants Pass, best known for his role in *Modern Family*.

FAERIEWORLDS

Faerieworlds is dubbed the "largest mythic, fantasy, and faerie-themed event in the U.S." The massive three-day music and art festival outside Portland is where festival-goers are inspired by the magic of music and beauty of things made by hand. Filled with costumes, exhibitions, and out-of-this-world cuisine, the festival is about celebrating the extraordinary to build new friendships and community.

TAMÁSTSLIKT CULTURAL INSTITUTE

Pendleton is home to this Indigenous peoples museum. It is run by the Cayuse, Umatilla, and Walla Walla tribes who have lived on the land for more than 10,000 years.

LEPRECHAUNS

Built in 1948, Mills End Park is home to a fabled group of invisible leprechauns, led by head leprechaun, Patrick O'Toole.

ROSE CITY

Portland's International Rose Test Garden grows over 600 varieties of rose. The Rose Festival hosts three big parades: the crowning of a queen, a carnival, and a treasure hunt, attracting nearly one million people annually.

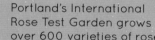

RETROGAMING EXPO

With old-school arcade games, free-play consoles, competitions, and more, Portland's Retro Gaming Expo is a gamer's paradise!

OTA TOFU

The oldest family-run tofu shop in America is in Portland. Founded in 1911, it marked an important moment in Japanese American history.

KID SCIENTISTS

Reed College in Portland is the only liberal arts college in the world with a nuclear reactor run by undergraduate students!

TECUMTUM
?–1864
The chief of the Etch-ka-taw-wah band of Athabaskan Indigenous Americans, who fought for the rights of southwestern Oregon tribal nations.

DOUGLAS CARL ENGELBART
1925–2013
Portland-born engineer and inventor who created the world's first computer mouse.

MOSES "BLACK" HARRIS
?–1849
Famed mountain man, fur trapper, explorer, and guide on the Oregon Trail, who became a legend for his contributions to the American development of the Pacific Northwest.

ANN CURRY
B.1956
This Japanese American, award-winning broadcast journalist, known for her coverage of humanitarian crises around the world, was raised in Oregon.

OREGON

PENNSYLV

QUAKERS
The Quakers fled religious persecution in England and founded the Pennsylvania colony. They organized the first religious protest against slavery in America in 1688. A Quaker community continues to live near Philadelphia.

ERIE

FURRY FANDOM
Hundreds of artists, animators, writers, costumers, and puppeteers celebrate their characters with parades, workshops, acting, and more at Anthrocon, a furry convention in Pittsburgh.

DUTCH FOLK
The legacy of the Pennsylvania Dutch—early German-speaking immigrants—is celebrated yearly at the nine-day Kutztown Folk Festival, where their art and cuisine are on display.

CHOCOLATETOWN
Hershey is the chocolate capital of the country! Hershey chocolate factories are the heart of the small town with the nation's largest chocolate factory.

ALLENTOWN

READING

STEEL CITY
Pittsburgh has a long history of steelmaking, which inspired the name for its football team, the Pittsburgh Steelers.

HARRISBURG

PHILADELPHIA

AMISH ANCESTRY
The Amish are known for simple living, plain dress, and avoidance of modern technology. Alongside the Mennonites and other small Christian sects, they were some of the first Europeans to settle the land.

PITTSBURGH

ANCIENT ROOTS
Indigenous heritage is celebrated by the Council of Three Rivers American Indian Center in Dorseyville in an annual powwow featuring singing, drumming, dancing, crafts, and Indigenous foods.

MUSHROOM MANIA
Pennsylvania produces more mushrooms than any other state! An annual mushroom festival takes place in Kennett Square.

THE ODUNDE FESTIVAL
This New Year celebration is the largest African American street festival in the country. It comes from the Yoruba people of Nigeria, but the festival is also a celebration of African, Caribbean, and Black heritage.

Archaeologists don't agree on when the first humans came to present-day Pennsylvania, but they've found artifacts dating back 19,400 years. Indigenous peoples such as the Lenape, Susquehannocks, Erie, Seneca, and Oneida lived on the land thousands of years later and well before the first Europeans, the Swedish and Dutch, arrived in 1638.

Nearly 50 years later, British colonists claimed the land. A wave of German-speaking immigrants, including Quakers, Mennonites, and Amish, followed soon after, fleeing religious intolerance, Although they came from all over Europe, their descendants are known today as Pennsylvania Dutch. In 1787, Pennsylvania became the second state to join the Union.

Pennsylvania is nicknamed the "Keystone State" because of its central location among the 13 original colonies. It made history as the home of Independence Hall, where the Declaration of Independence and the U.S. Constitution were drafted. Chocolate, cheesesteaks, pretzels, and the world-renowned artistic and musical hub of Philadelphia are just a few of the delights to have been born in Pennsylvania.

ANIA

KOBE BRYANT
1978–2020
Philly-born professional basketball player and the third all-time leading scorer, regarded as one of the greatest players of all time.

TINA FEY
B.1970
Award-winning comedian, actor, writer, and producer from Upper Derby.

SCOTT FAHLMAN
B.1948
In 1982, this Carnegie Mellon University professor invented the first Internet emoticon, the smiley.

KEY FACTS

CAPITAL CITY
Harrisburg

TOTAL POPULATION OF STATE
13,002,700

AREA OF STATE (SQ MI)
46,054

POPULATION OF CAPITAL
50,099

HISPANIC HEARTS
The 222 Latino Corridor, or Corazón de la Comunidad, which gets it's name from route 222, has the state's largest Latino population with roots in more than a dozen different countries and cultures.

THE LENAPE
The Lenni-Lenape were the first known Philly residents. Thousands of Lenape still live in the city, which celebrates its cultural ancestors through a massive annual cultural festival and awareness campaign called Indigenous Peoples' Day.

BLACK COWBOYS
For over a century, Black equestrians at Fletcher Street Urban Riding Club have cared for horses and provided lessons to Philadelphia's youth.

COMPUTER GENIUSES
One of the world's first computers—the Electronic Numerical Integrator and Computer—was invented at the University of Pennsylvania in 1946. It weighed 28 tons!

THE CITY OF BROTHERLY LOVE
Philadelphia earns its nickname from the religious tolerance of William Penn, the state's founder. It was one of the first cities to guarantee religious freedom to all its immigrants.

TAMANEND
C.1625–1701
Chief of the Turtle Clan of the Lenni-Lenape nation, Tamanend signed a peace treaty with William Penn in 1683.

WILL SMITH
B.1968
West Philadelphia-native actor, rapper, and film producer who became a millionaire before he turned 20 years old.

PENNSYLVANIAN TASTE BUDS
Pennsylvanians handmade pretzels originated with German settlers. The state is also known for whoopie pies and Philly cheesesteaks.

MECCA OF THE WEST
Muslims make up a dynamic community in Philadelphia. In the 1920s, the Nation of Islam set up temples across the city. Over time, the Black congregation became orthodox Muslims. The community diversified with converts and immigrants from every race and culture. Islam became an integral part of local music culture, influencing jazz, rap, and hip-hop artists, and continues to do so today. Today, Philadelphia is often referred to as the "Mecca of the West." There are streets lined with Muslim-owned businesses, an Islamic history museum, and many Muslim community organizations and charitable initiatives. Muslim culture is mainstream, from the popular saying of "what's up ach?" ("brother" in Arabic) to the global beard trend known as the Philly beard.

DOUGHNUT LOVERS
Providence has more doughnut shops per person than anywhere else in the country.

CAPE VERDEAN AMERICANS
Rhode Island has the largest Cape Verdean community in the U.S. Providence holds the oldest celebration of the Cape Verdean community in an annual festival.

JHUMPA LAHIRI
B.1967
Indian American author, most well known for her Pulitzer Prize-winning collection of short stories, *Interpreter of Maladies*.

SAM BERNS
1996–2014
Born with a condition called progeria, Berns became a local and national hero for his work raising awareness about the rare disorder.

BUDDING ARTISTS
The Rhode Island School of Design (RISD) was one of the first art schools in the country. The RISD Museum is home to world-class paintings, sculptures, and photography.

PAWTUCKET

GUN SAFETY ADVOCATES
The Gun Totem is a 12-foot, 3,500-pound obelisk made with more than 1,000 fossilized guns! It was part of a program to get guns off the streets.

PROVIDENCE

CRANSTON

WARWICK

THE FIRST JEWS
The Touro Synagogue in Newport, built in the 1760s, is the oldest remaining synagogue in North America and houses the oldest Torah in the country.

AFRICAN AMERICAN SOLDIERS
The Dexter Training Ground was where the Union Army's Black Civil War troops trained. The first African American military regiment was the 1st Rhode Island Regiment.

GOD'S LITTLE ACRE
This cemetery is the oldest and largest surviving collection of grave markers of enslaved and free Africans—the earliest is from the 1600s.

SCUBA DIVERS
Fort Wetherill is a former coast artillery fort-turned-park. Its walking trails along the rocky coast end in a popular destination for scuba diving.

NEWPORT

PRINCESS RED WING
1896–1987
A Narragansett and Wampanoag elder and internationally known activist who fought for her nation's rights after the Indian Reorganization Act was passed.

DIY-ERS
Old barns in Charlestown were repurposed into the Fantastic Umbrella Factory, a site for DIY hobbyists.

NARRAGANSETT NATION
This tribal nation is descended from Rhode Island's first inhabitants, who lived more than 30,000 years ago!

GHOST HOSTS
Belcourt Castle is supposedly haunted. In 1891, it was accidentally built over graves and many ghosts are said to live within its walls.

ALL THAT JAZZ
Famous jazz musicians including Duke Ellington, Miles Davis, and Ella Fitzgerald have all performed in the country's oldest annual jazz event, the Newport Jazz Festival.

KEY FACTS

CAPITAL CITY
Providence

TOTAL POPULATION OF STATE
1,097,379

AREA OF STATE (SQ MI)
1,545

POPULATION OF CAPITAL
190,934

CARNIVAL-GOERS
Watch Hill boasts the nation's oldest flying horses carousel, which has been in continuous operation since 1867.

AHOY, PIRATES!
Block Island is a small island off the southern coast of Rhode Island, rumored to have been a pirate hideout.

Rhode Island

LIZZIE MURPHY
1894–1964
Known as the "Queen of Baseball," she was the first woman to play professional baseball, competing with male athletes.

DR. RAYMOND T. JACKSON
B.1933
Accomplished concert pianist and the first African American musician, and youngest person, to be elected into the Rhode Island Heritage Hall of Fame.

On the northeastern American coast sits its smallest state, Rhode Island. It was home first to many Indigenous groups who helped shape the region we know today. When European colonizers arrived, the main nations were the Pequots, Nipmucs, Niantics, Narragansetts, and Wampanoags. In 1636, the British claimed it as a colony. But Rhode Island has a reputation for being revolutionary. It was the first to abolish slavery, the first to reject British rule, and the first to sign a bill of rights for people who are homeless. In 1790 it officially became a U.S. state.

Today, Rhode Island is small in size but dense in population. The "Ocean State" is famous the world over as the sailing capital of the world. It is also known for being a hub of shipping and trade, producing fine coffee, milk, and jewelry, and being home to the world's largest (fake) bug.

THE WAMPANOAG NATION
A confederation of Indigenous groups from Rhode Island, known for their beadwork. Their use of the quahog, or hard clam, in food, wampum jewelry, and trade may have inspired Rhode Island's famous New England clam chowder.

THE PROVIDENCE WATERFIRE
The Providence WaterFire is a dazzling art installation made of fire. Volunteers sail down the river, lighting more than 100 floating bonfires for the event. The string of blazes illuminates nearly 1 mile of urban spaces along the river, where visitors can enjoy food and performances by firelight.

MARY McLEOD BETHUNE
1987–1955
An educator and civil rights activist, Bethune started a private school for African American students that would develop into Bethune-Cookman University.

CHUBBY CHECKER
B.1941
A rock and roll singer and dancer, best known for popularizing dance styles of the 1960s, including "the twist."

JAMES E. CLYBURN
B.1940
Clyburn has served as the U.S. Representative for South Carolina's 6th Congressional District since 1993.

VIOLA DAVIS
B.1965
The youngest person and first African American to earn the "Triple Crown of Acting" honor.

ROCK HILL

CATAWBA NATION
The Catawba nation once dominated the area with an estimate of up to 25,000 members. Today the nation is smaller, but federally recognized in the state, and teaches its culture through education and handmade jewelry.

MILLION MAN MARCH TRIBUTE
In 2020 thousands of people from across the nation marched from Five Points to the Columbia statehouse as tribute to the 1995 Million Man March. It was a march to promote positive images of Black men and social justice in Washington, D.C.

WEDDING BELLS
Young couples take a ride down Highway 501 near Myrtle Beach to visit a tiny church, called the Traveler's Chapel, which is one of the state's most popular wedding destinations.

HIKE TO THE TOP
In the Blue Ridge portion of the Appalachian Mountains, Sassafras Mountain is the highest point in the state of South Carolina and attracts hundreds of locals and visitors each year.

SIKH COMMUNITY
The Sikh Religious Society of South Carolina is in Chapin and provides a community that extends beyond the town. Sikh families from all over the state gather on the third Sunday of the month to worship together.

HISPANIC COMMUNITY
Saluda County has a large community of Hispanic Americans. The population is composed of diverse cultures from various countries like the Caribbean, Puerto Rico, and South America.

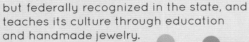

SALUDA COUNTY

COLUMBIA

TURKISH ROOTS
Sumter County is home to a group of Turkish residents who can trace their roots back to the Revolutionary War!

MODJESKA MONTEITH SIMKINS
1899–1992
Simkins was an African American leader in public health and social reform. She was also involved in the civil rights movement in South Carolina.

GOOD ROLLIN' FUN
St. George hosts the World Grits Festival. The Rolling in the Grits contest sees competitors roll around in grits to see who can stick as much as possible on their body!

NORTH CHARLESTON

MOUNT PLEASANT

CHARLESTON

Taking its nickname from the state's tree, the "Palmetto State" has a history as colorful as the lovely terrain. South Carolina became the eighth state in the Union on May 23, 1788. During the Revolutionary War, South Carolina hosted a great deal of the conflict. About a third of combat took place here, which is more than any other state. South Carolina has three main geographic regions: the Atlantic coastal plain (home to the state's well-known beaches), the plateau region called the Piedmont, and the Blue Ridge Mountains.

South Carolina is a diverse state. Charleston has a high concentration of African Americans that speak the Gullah language, and there is a diverse population of Latino and Asian cultures. As the state continues to become more mixed, new residents have a choice of beautiful landscapes and amazing culture.

GULLAH LOVE
Gullah Geechee people, who live near the coastal area and islands, are a historic group of Black people with unique food, customs, and a language that upholds their African roots.

TEA GROWERS
Residents of Wadmalaw Island, off the coast, enjoy access to the largest producer of tea in the U.S. The Charleston Tea Garden produces over 300 varieties of tea!

SOUTH CAROLINA

KEY FACTS

CAPITAL CITY
Columbia

TOTAL POPULATION OF STATE
5,118,425

AREA OF STATE (SQ MI)
32,020

POPULATION OF CAPITAL
136,632

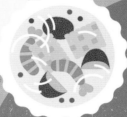

MOTHER EMANUEL
Known as the earliest African Methodist Episcopal church in the South, this church also has one of the oldest congregations and is a national historic site.

LOW-COUNTRY BOIL
People in the southeast area of the state have popularized a one-pot meal called the "Low-Country boil." This celebrated dish includes seafood, corn, and sausage, all boiled together and served by pouring it on a covered table for folks to dig in!

BOOKS, Y'ALL!
YALLFest, a festival celebrating young adult books, is a two-day event that brings readers and authors together. It's the largest teen book festival in the world, with over 70 authors and 12,000 book lovers!

AFRICAN AMERICAN HISTORIC SITE
Residents of Charleston remember the sacrifices of enslaved Africans at the International African American Museum.

The Historic
MYRTLE BEACH COLORED SCHOOL
Museum & Education Center

MYRTLE BEACH SCHOOL MUSEUM
Residents of Myrtle Beach pay homage to an all-Black school that taught students during segregation. Today the school serves as a museum to teach the community about its past.

OYOTUNJI AFRICAN VILLAGE
Founded in 1970, Oyotunji African Village is a community based on Nigerian Yoruba culture. The village was founded by the priest Adefunmi in 1970, who named it after the Yoruba kingdom of Oyo; "Oyotunji" means "Oyo rises again." The village was founded to establish a religious and cultural community for African Americans who practiced the Yoruba faith. Today the Oyotunji African Village continues to promote Yoruba history and culture by hosting art shows and educational programs, as well as festivals, books, films, and spiritual services for the community.

OYOTUNJI

FOREFATHERS' MONUMENT

South Dakota is known for the colossal Mount Rushmore, a sculpture carved into the granite of the Black Hills. The sculpture features the 60-foot heads of four U.S. presidents—George Washington, Thomas Jefferson, Theodore Roosevelt, and Abraham Lincoln. The presidents chosen for Mount Rushmore represent the birth (Washington), growth (Jefferson), development (Roosevelt), and preservation (Lincoln) of the nation. Over two million people visit this monument each year. However, it is not without controversy. The Black Hills are a sacred site to the local Lakota Sioux people, and had been promised to them in a treaty with the U.S. government. To some, the monument is a painful reminder of the land that was taken from them.

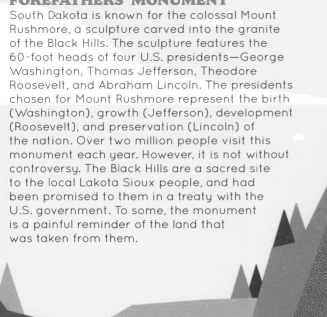

TERRY REDLIN
1937–2016
Once named America's most popular artist, Redlin is known for painting outdoor scenes of rural bliss and wildlife, often pictured in twilight.

MARY GRANDPRÉ
B.1954
Illustrator best known for her cover and chapter illustrations of the U.S. editions of the *Harry Potter* books.

STEPPING INTO THE FUTURE
Once home to thousands of mining families, the city of Lead has made a name for itself as a center of science with its underground laboratory. Here scientists study engineering and biology.

GOLDEN VIEWS
Early settlers rushed to South Dakota for its gold. Today, the state is still the leading producer of gold, valued at more than $1 billion.

BLAST FROM THE PAST
Honoring the first pioneers that arrived in 1876, the Days of '76 Rodeo in Deadwood is a historic celebration honoring the Old West! Join residents as they host an outdoor rodeo and Indigenous culture celebrations.

BIKERS' PARADISE
Over 500,000 bikers and bike enthusiasts gather each year for the ten-day Sturgis Motorcycle Rally.

ENTER THE BADLANDS
Archaeologists and dinosaur enthusiasts gather in the western part of the state, called the Badlands, because it's a hotspot for ancient animal fossils. A saber-toothed cat and even a prehistoric rhino have been found!

LEAD

RAPID CITY

HIKER'S TRAIL
Every year, nearly 13,000 people take part in an organized 6-mile trail to the Crazy Horse Memorial, which honors the famed Lakota war leader.

INDIGENOUS POP ART
Residents in Rapid City host an art show and shop featuring Indigenous art. Visitors can support Indigenous artists in their area by purchasing art from local artists.

OGLALA NATION POWWOW
One of the oldest Indigenous groups in the state, the Oglala keep their traditions alive by hosting an annual powwow and rodeo where visitors can learn more about their history and culture.

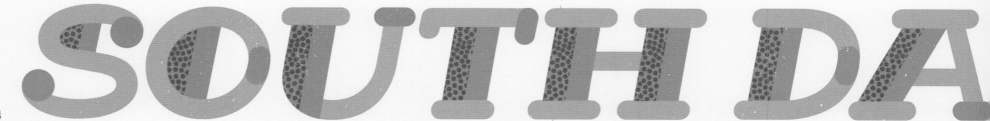
SOUTH DA

KEY FACTS

CAPITAL CITY
Pierre

TOTAL POPULATION OF STATE
886,667

AREA OF STATE (SQ MI)
77,116

POPULATION OF CAPITAL
14,091

OSCAR HOWE
1915-1983
An Indigenous American artist, Howe was well known for his unique tempera paintings.

Known for its tourism and agriculture, South Dakota is a state brimming with possibilities. The Lakota and Dakota Sioux span this area and North Dakota. The vast plains area was once one large mass until the government divided it into two regions. South Dakota became a state in 1889, along with its sister state, North Dakota. While most of the European population settled in the eastern area, Indigenous Americans dominated the western part of the state, where ranching became a huge business.

Today, the state has become a large tourist destination. Millions of people visit Mount Rushmore for the presidential monument, and the Badlands, where some of the oldest fossils have been discovered. With a strong Old West culture in historic cities like Deadwood, South Dakota is a state that prides itself on its rural lifestyle and agriculture.

ABERDEEN

BUFFALO ROUNDUP
Residents can watch cowboys and cowgirls round up a herd of 1,300 buffalo in Pierre.

LITTLE PIONEER
Fans of the popular pioneer Laura Ingalls Wilder flock to De Smet for an annual celebration of prairie culture, featuring outdoor family-friendly plays based on Wilder's writings.

WATERTOWN

LAURA INGALLS WILDER
1867-1957
The author of the *Little House* series gained fame by writing about her adventures on the South Dakota prairie.

VINE VICTOR DELORIA JR.
1933-2005
An author and activist, Deloria is known for attracting national attention to Indigenous American issues through his writing.

BROOKINGS

PADDLING THE MIGHTY MO'
This state's outdoor enthusiasts love kayaking, canoeing, or paddling down the long Missouri River, known as the "Mighty Mo!"

PIERRE

SIOUX FALLS

CZECH DAYS IN TABOR
Celebrating their Czech roots, residents in Tabor host a cultural festival where you can learn about Czech history and how to bake special dishes like kolaches—sweet-dough pastries with a fruit filling.

BUTTERFLY KINGDOM
Butterfly enthusiasts flock to South Dakota to study more than 175 different butterfly species, such as the American lady and cabbage white butterflies.

THE INDIGENOUS NATION
The Lakota, Western Dakota, and Eastern Dakota make up the Sioux Nation, an Indigenous group that has lived in the state for hundreds of years.

SIOUX EMPIRE
Locals flock to Sioux Falls for the annual Sioux Empire Fair, where they can socialize, play games, and watch the big rodeo!

CAPITAL CITY
Nashville

TOTAL POPULATION OF STATE
6,910,840

AREA OF STATE (SQ MI)
42,144

POPULATION OF CAPITAL
689,447

Known for its beautiful valleys and tree-covered ridges, Tennessee is the 16th state, joining the Union on June 1, 1796. The name "Tennessee" derives from a Cherokee village in the area called "Tenasi." Cherokee were dominant in the area before European settlers arrived. Years later, during the Civil War, the region was torn between Confederate and northern sympathizers. Eventually, the state was the last to secede from the Union and the first to be admitted again once the war was over. The diverse landscape is dominated by cotton, corn, and soybeans.

Today the state is known for its food, history, and music. Nashville is known as "Music City" and the country-music capital of the world. The Grand Ole Opry, the longest-running radio broadcast and music show in U.S. history, also calls the state home. Blues and gospel are a big part of music history in Memphis. With roots steeped in history, Tennessee is a state where music and culture combine.

ISRAELI CELEBRATION
The Israeli community in Memphis hosts an annual festival to promote and celebrate their culture. Visitors can learn more about famous Israeli people, places, and food.

MEMPHIS ITALIANS
Italian culture is celebrated in Memphis with the Italian Festival, an annual weekend event that includes Italian traditions like grape-stomping, and fun activities such as volleyball tournaments.

HENRY CHO
B.1962
An American comedian, Cho is known for his appearances on the Grand Ole Opry weekly country music concert.

NATIONAL CIVIL RIGHTS MUSEUM
History buffs flock to the popular National Civil Rights Museum, built around the old Lorraine Motel, the site of the assassination of Dr. Martin Luther King, Jr., in Memphis. The museum follows the history of the civil rights movement up to the present day.

BELZ MUSEUM of Asian & Judaic Art

BELZ MUSEUM OF ASIAN AND JUDAIC ART
Fans of unique art can head down to Memphis to view 1,000 works and art objects created by Judaic and Asian artists. Some pieces are over 2,000 years old.

MUSIC STARS
Singers and musicians flock to Music City, also known as Nashville, in hopes of becoming America's next star. Nashville streets are filled with singers and music lounges featuring spotlit hopefuls.

NASHVILLE CROSSROADS "MUSIC CITY"

CLARKSVILLE

NASHVILLE

SUMMER AVENUE FOOD
Locals boast that this 6-mile avenue is home to the best food in the state! Chefs from different cultures create delicious meals and treats, like snow cones and breakfast biscuits. From barbecue to Thai food, this area has the best of the best!

ROCKABILLY
The Rockabilly Hall of Fame honors influential acts, such as Gene Vincent, in the music genre of rockabilly (a blend of country, rhythm and blues, bluegrass, and rock and roll). The museum attracts hundreds of visitors annually.

FARM LIFE
Tennessee farmers provide fuel and food not only to its residents but the rest of the country. Some 75% of the farmland is reserved for corn, hay, and cotton—the top crops in the state.

MEOWS HOUSE
If you love cats, head to Memphis to visit the House of Mews, a cat adoption agency. Cats roam freely throughout the building, so be careful not to let one out when you open the door!

SCHOOLHOUSE ROCK
Fans of rock star Tina Turner can visit the exact place she went to school. The one-room schoolhouse attended by Turner as a child was turned into a museum in her honor. Visitors can see old pictures and memorabilia relating to the superstar.

MEMPHIS

4E 97
ORANGE MOUND

ORANGE MOUND PRIDE
One of the earliest neighborhoods in Memphis to be built by and for African Americans, residents of Orange Mound keep their history alive with an oral history project, where elders share stories and history.

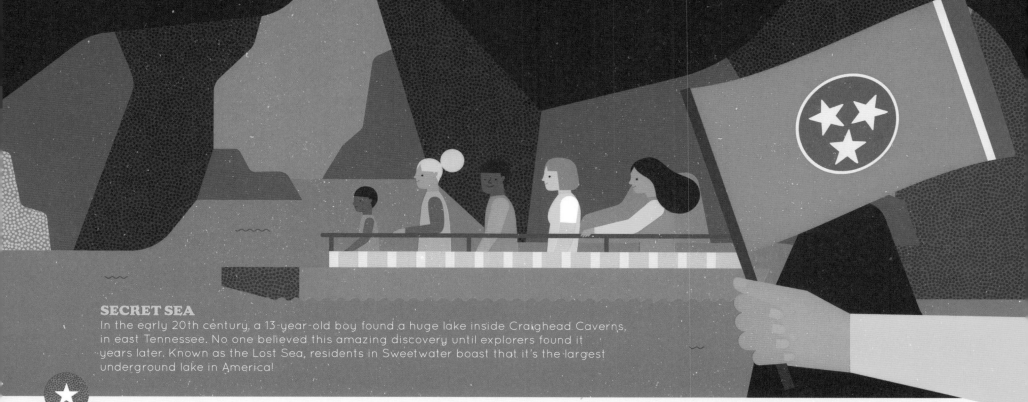

SECRET SEA

In the early 20th century, a 13-year-old boy found a huge lake inside Craighead Caverns, in east Tennessee. No one believed this amazing discovery until explorers found it years later. Known as the Lost Sea, residents in Sweetwater boast that it's the largest underground lake in America!

DOLLY PARTON
B.1946

Known for her work as a country music artist, Dolly Parton used that success to also advance as an actor, businesswoman, and humanitarian, among other endeavors.

CHEROKEE DAYS

The Knoxville area was home to many Cherokees before the settlers pushed them out. Residents honor their heritage every summer with dance demonstrations, food, and unique crafts.

MARY CHURCH TERRELL
1863–1954

A national civil rights activist and one of the first African American woman to earn a college degree. She also taught at the M Street school, the first African American public high school in the U.S.

MAURICE WHITE
1941–2016

An inductee of the Rock and Roll Hall of Fame, White was also the leader of the pop/funk band Earth, Wind & Fire.

BIBLE BELT

Tennessee is in the heart of the "Bible Belt," a group of heavily Christian states. A total of 82% of Tennessee residents are Christian.

KNOXVILLE

ATHENS OF THE SOUTH

Visitors head to Knoxville for Greek Fest, which celebrates Greek culture and heritage in the state. The local Greek community enjoys traditional dancing and authentic food.

THELMA HARPER
1940–2021

The first African American female state senator for Tennessee, Harper was also the state's longest-serving female senator, holding the position from 1989–2018.

DANCE OF THE FIREFLIES

Gatlinburg locals are in for a treat every June. For two weeks, fireflies in the Smoky Mountains perform a beautiful light show in the evenings!

CHATTANOOGA

tennessee

This great state boasts large cities and country towns, dusty deserts, and grassy hills. In the early 1700s, Spanish missionaries settled in Texas and founded the city of San Antonio in 1718. Texas was a Mexican province after Mexico gained independence from Spain, but tensions between the Mexican population, the incoming European settlers, and Indigenous people led to several uprisings. The Texas Revolution of 1835 saw the state become an independent nation, and is the reason for its modern-day nickname, "The Lone Star State." However, the Texas Republic was unable to defend itself against Mexican troops, and in 1845, Texas joined the U.S. as the 28th state.

Since then, Texas has become a melting pot of culture and heritage. As the second largest U.S. state, it's known for its big personality— big trucks, big hats, and big fun! Mexican heritage remains a huge influence on Texas culture. This unique cultural mix has given the world Tex-Mex food as well as Tejano music and dance.

SELENA
1971–1995
Known as the "Queen of Tejano music," Selena Perez was an influential singer, songwriter, and one of the best-selling female artists in Latin music.

COWGIRL HISTORY
Wild West lovers unite in Amarillo! The history of women in Western culture is on full display down the historic Route 66.

THE VAQUEROS
Vaqueros were the first Western cowboys. They rode horses and corralled livestock. Their style remains a part of Texas's culture.

EL PASO

TEX-MEX FOODIES
Food lovers come to Texas for its unique cuisine: a blend of Texan and Mexican styles of cooking called Tex-Mex. Its signature ingredient is cheese—lots of it.

BLACK SEMINOLES
This group of freedmen and Indigenous Americans expanded across the South and some served as U.S. Army Scouts. Brackettville hosts celebrations and has a historic cemetery in their honor.

THE KICKAPOO PEOPLE
This traditional tribe is known for their farming customs. Living near the Mexico border, Kickapoo people continue to keep their heritage alive.

SOUTH BY SOUTHWEST
South by Southwest is an Austin mega-festival that features film, media, and music. This annual festival is one of the largest creative gatherings in the world. Notable speakers and performers have included President Barack Obama and First Lady Michelle Obama. The festival has also become a place to unveil new technology. In 2019, a medical pen that easily detects cancerous tissue was unveiled. Thousands stand in line to be the first to view the latest gadgets and medical technology.

SXSW

ROPIN' AND RIDIN'
An ode to Texas's Old West roots, the Stockyards Championship Rodeo attracts rodeo enthusiasts year round. Here cowboys show their skills in a series of contests.

MARSAI MARTIN
B.2004
A Plano native, this award-winning actor is also a producer.

DORIS MILLER
1919–1943
Miller was the first Black American to be awarded the Navy Cross for his courage during the 1941 attack on Pearl Harbor.

CAPITAL CITY
Austin

TOTAL POPULATION OF STATE
29,145,505

AREA OF STATE (SQ MI)
268,596

POPULATION OF CAPITAL
961,855

DEEP ELLUM ARTISTS
Historically a cultural center for Black Americans, Deep Ellum is home to a diverse group of artists and an annual arts festival.

DALLAS

FORT WORTH

WILD WEST FOLKLORE
People who love Texas history can join the folklore society, where monsters, myths, and legends are gathered and shared.

TASTE OF THAI
The Thai Culture and Food Festival is a two-day event in downtown Dallas celebrating the state's Thai culture.

PIT MASTERS
Austin is famous for its barbecue. People from all over stand in line for hours at local restaurants for a taste of their smoky meat.

TEXAN DEVILS
An Austin-based law enforcement agency, the Texas Ranger Division, became cultural icons due to their historic run-ins with outlaws.

AUSTIN

SAN ANTONIO

HOUSTON

BUFFALO SOLDIERS
This African American military regiment protected frontier settlements and mapped Texas. Tourists learn more about the group at their Houston museum.

JUNETEENTH
A national holiday, people celebrate June 19 as the day enslaved people in Galveston learned they were free in 1865. They were one of the last groups of slaves to be freed.

BATTY WATCHERS
One of Austin's favorite pastimes, tourists can go on bat-watching tours throughout the city.

ENCHANTED ROCKERS
Rock climbers and campers travel to Fredericksburg to hike up the large, pink granite mountain.

DEBBIE ALLEN
B.1950
An award-winning actor, Allen is also a choreographer, director, and producer.

JUDITH ZAFFIRINI
B.1946
The first Mexican American woman elected to the Texas Senate, Zaffirini was once named one of the Top 100 most influential Hispanics in the United States.

TEXAS

DUTCH BAKERS
One of Utah's official state symbols is the Dutch oven. The cast-iron cooking pots were lifesavers for westbound pioneers who traveled across great expanses of land. These pots made cooking while traveling much easier.

MORMONS
Almost 70% of Utah identifies as Mormon—that's more than two million people!

MODERN-DAY MUMMIES
Summum is a unique religion. It blends science fiction, mysticism, and ancient religions. Based in Salt Lake City, they practice modern mummification with plans to clone themselves in the future.

REPUBLIC OF ZAQISTAN
A micro-nation in the middle of Utah created in 2005, this republic is called home by a handful of people and artists for a few days every year.

Welcome to
THE REPUBLIC OF
ZAQISTAN

SALT LAKE CITY

SPIDER LOVERS
Every year, Antelope Island crawls with millions of spiders! The annual Spider Fest helps locals identify various species.

WEST VALLEY CITY

WEST JORDAN

LGBTQ+
Salt Lake City is one of the most queer-friendly cities in America! The Utah Pride Festival is one of the largest and longest running in the country.

BLACK UTAH
Utah is home to one of the smallest populations of Black people. However, Salt Lake City has created the Black Lives Matter History Bus and Mobile Museum to celebrate Black history.

COWBOY POETS
Heber Valley Western Music and Cowboy Poetry Gathering is the largest cowboy poetry event in the country! Through music and guitar-playing, poets share stories of cowboy culture.

OREM

PROVO

UTE PEOPLE
The Uintah and Ouray reservation is the second-largest reservation in the country. It is home to the Southern Utes, including the White Mesa Utes, and the Diné people, commonly known as Navajos.

SUNDANCE MOVIEMAKERS
Up-and-coming moviemakers head to the Sundance Film Festival every year to showcase their new movies. It is the biggest independent film festival in the country.

JACKIE BISKUPSKI
B.1966
American politician who became mayor of Salt Lake City and the city's first openly gay mayor.

STATE FORESTERS
Utah is the only state where every county contains some part of a national forest. It has an extensive network of preservationists who team up to keep the forests safe and healthy.

MARS EXPLORERS
Members of the Mars Desert Research Station (MDRS) in the San Rafael Swell have been preparing for a manned mission to Mars. They use local terrain to mimic alien worlds.

SLICKROCK MOUNTAIN BIKING
Mountain bikers come from around the world to ride over the reddish-orange Navajo Sandstone on the world-famous Slickrock Trail.

WAKARA
C.1815–1855
Legendary Timpanogo leader born near the Spanish Fork River. He was known as a skilled horseman and for resolving conflict with invading Mormons.

LITTLE HOLLYWOOD
Kane County has served as the backdrop for dozens of movies. From the 1920s on, it's been the perfect spot for filmmakers of Westerns, such as *The Lone Ranger*.

FRANK ZAMBONI
1901–1988
Born in Eureka, he invented the ice-resurfacing machine called the Zamboni, used to clear ice for skating and hockey.

TERRY TEMPEST WILLIAMS
B.1955
Writer, educator, and conservationist who focuses on social and environmental justice.

ANCESTRAL PUEBLOAN RUINS
The Anasazi inhabitants created a unique 90-room structure tucked beneath a desert cliff. Today, it's a unique window into the lives of Southwestern Indigenous Americans who lived nearly 1,000 years ago.

WALTER FREDERICK MORRISON
1920–2010
Inventor of the frisbee which he first called "Pluto Platters."

UTAH

CAPITAL CITY
Salt Lake City

TOTAL POPULATION OF STATE
3,271,616

AREA OF STATE (SQ MI)
84,897

POPULATION OF CAPITAL
199,723

Indigenous people including the ancient Puebloans, the Navajo, and the Ute have lived in Utah for thousands of years. The Spanish were the first Europeans to arrive in the 1500s, claiming it as a part of New Spain and later Mexico. Americans, most notably Mormons fleeing persecution, settled in the area as well. After the Mexican–American War, Utah was admitted into the Union as the 45th state in 1896. Its name comes from the Ute word for mountain people.

Owing to its central location among the western states, Utah has earned the nickname "Crossroads of the West." It is the second-driest state in the country and its Great Salt Lake is believed to be the largest saltwater lake in the Western Hemisphere. Today, members of the Bannock, Goshute, Navajo, Paiute, Shoshone, and Ute tribal nations continue to live on their ancestral lands. Utah is also known as a worldwide center for Mormonism, a universal destination for skiing, and a place filled with natural wonders, from breathtaking national parks to the fossilised remains of dinosaurs.

TEMPLE OF COLOR
Spanish Fork hosts the largest Holi festival in the Western Hemisphere. The Sri Sri Radha Krishna Temple draws thousands of people to the Festival of Colors to enjoy music, get covered in colored powder, and celebrate Holi every year!

SNOWBOARD LEGENDS

Burlington local, Jake Burton, a former ski racer, was inspired by snurfing. He is one of the inventors of the modern-day snowboard.

SNOWFLAKE PHOTOGRAPHERS

Vermonter Wilson Bentley, a farmer, invented a unique technique to capture snowflake images. He discovered that no two flakes are the same.

THE ABENAKI

The Nulhegan Abenaki are one of the largest Abenaki tribes still in existence today. They continue to promote their nomadic culture and celebrate their heritage in their traditional homeland called N'dakinna, which includes Vermont.

BOSNIAN VERMONTERS

Burlington residents help Bosnians who fled war in the 1990s. They celebrate their heritage with the Bosnian Vermont Film Festival and the Bosnian Lilies Dancing Group, who weave and whirl through crowds to traditional Bosnian music.

CHEESY FARMERS

Cabot Creamery, owned by local dairy farmers, holds the record for the world's largest grilled cheese sandwich. The sandwich weighed 320 pounds and was more than 10 feet long!

COLCHESTER

ESSEX

BURLINGTON ◄ SOUTH BURLINGTON

WONDERFUL WEB SITE

Knight's Spider Web Farm has a collection of more than 16,000 webs from orb-weaver spiders. Farmers preserve and sell the arachnid masterpieces.

MONTPELIER

ROCK CARVERS

The Rock of Ages is the world's largest operating deep-hole granite quarry. There is even a granite bowling lane that visitors can try!

MOO ENGLAND

Vermont's farmers run nearly half of the dairy farms in New England!

BEE YOURSELF

Vermonters are not afraid of a little sting! The state's beekeepers help keep the honey industry buzzing. Now, this popular hobby has turned into a full-blow sustainability project.

THE SWEET LIFE

Vermont is the largest producer of maple syrup in the U.S., producing over 1.5 million gallons a year. It takes 40 gallons of sap to produce a single gallon of syrup, so savor every drop!

WORLD OF STEAMPUNK

At Springfield's Steampunk Festival, fans find three days of trader's bazaars, walking history tours, candlepin bowling tournaments, and much more. Spend some time in this futuristic yesteryear!

RUTLAND CITY

MARVELOUS MARBLERS

The Danby Quarry is the world's largest underground marble quarry in the world. At one point more than 200 workers, equipped with diamond-tipped saws, cut stone from the mountain.

SNOW GOLFERS

Snow golf was invented in Dummerston by the *Jungle Book* author, Rudyard Kipling.

AFRICAN AMERICAN HERITAGE TRAIL

A unique historical trip takes you along the state's legacy of Black Americans, including a stop in Grafton—a town of 670 people—where visitors learn about former slave Alec Turner, who settled there in 1872.

ORGAN PLAYERS

Estey Organ Museum is filled with humming, wheezing, and whining. The museum is dedicated to the town's organ factory, which produced more than half a million organs to be sent around the world.

STROLLING OF THE HEIFERS PARADE

Brattleboro hosts the summertime Strolling of the Heifers parade which celebrates Vermont's dairy culture. Although inspired by Spain's Running of the Bulls, the stroll is a procession of friendly, ambling heifer calves, groomed to the nines. They are colorfully bedecked with hats and flowers, and led by future farmers. It's a celebration of family farmers, local food, and rural life!

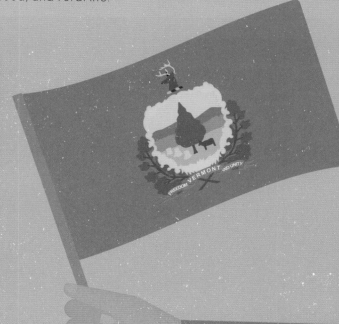

The history of Indigenous peoples in Vermont stretches back to 8500 BCE. Between 1000 BCE and 1600 CE, parts of the region were inhabited by the Abenaki and Mohican peoples. Around 1500, the Haudenosaunee alliance expanded into the area and drove out many of the smaller groups. In the 1600s, the French claimed the territory as part of New France before the British took it over in 1763. In 1777, Vermont declared itself an independent republic, and was the first North American colony to abolish slavery. It became the 14th U.S. state in 1791.

Vermont is today known for its forests, covered bridges, and ski slopes. It has the smallest state capital and one of the lowest populations in the nation. Vermont is famous for foods like cheddar cheese, maple syrup, and ice cream, alongside its historic textile industry and picturesque scenery, perfect for outdoor adventures.

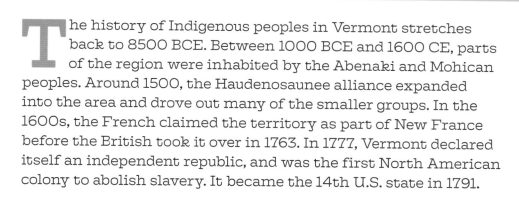

ALEXANDER TWILIGHT
1795-1857
The first known African American to graduate from college in the United States.

PATTY SHEEHAN
B.1956
Professional golf champion and member of the World Golf Hall of Fame.

JOHN DEERE
1804-1886
Founder of a gardening equipment empire. He invented the first commercially successful steel plow.

BERNIE SANDERS
B.1941
No-nonsense politician, activist, and legislator who is also the longest-serving independent in U.S. congressional history.

ANDREW ELLICOTT DOUGLASS
1867-1962
Astronomer who founded dendrochronology, which is a method of dating wood by analyzing its growth ring pattern.

Vermont

VIRGINIA

As the site of both the first British colony in North America and the last battle fought in the American Revolution, Virginia has seen its fair share of history. The original home of the Powhatan people, the state is known as the birthplace of the nation. It was one of the 13 colonies during the American Revolution, and became a state in 1776. During the Civil War, Virginians couldn't agree on which side to fight for. This caused western counties to separate from the state and form another: West Virginia. Virginia went through a recovery period after the devastation of the Civil War, half of which was fought on Virginian soil. Plantation owners had to learn how to manage farmland without enslaved labor.

Today, Virginia is popular for its varied geography that stretches from western forests and rivers to low-lying swamps in the east. Historically a center for coal mining, Virginia continues to attract new residents with its pioneering technology and defense industries. It is one of the most diverse states in the South. With beautiful beaches, mountain views, and famous Smithfield ham, Virginia remains a jewel of the South and of the east coast.

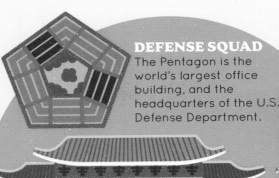

DEFENSE SQUAD
The Pentagon is the world's largest office building, and the headquarters of the U.S. Defense Department.

EDEN CENTER
Northern Virginia boasts Eden Center, a shopping mall that has been home to Vietnamese American businesses for more than 30 years.

SECRET AGENTS
Virginia is home to the Central Intelligence Agency, which employs over 20,000 people.

MISSY ELLIOTT
B.1971
Hailed as the best-selling female rapper in history, Missy is known for her eclectic style.

POET'S PLAYHOUSE
Fans of Shakespeare love Blackfriars Playhouse, a faithful recreation of the Bard's favored Blackfriars theater, in London, U.K.

YOUNG TECHIES
Over 25,000 students study at Virginia Tech due to its focus on technology careers.

MARY JACKSON
1921–2005
This mathematician became NASA's first African American female engineer.

CONSTANCE WU
B.1982
Known for her role in *Crazy Rich Asians*, Wu is an influential actor.

GABBY DOUGLAS
B.1995
This high-flying, history-making gymnast is the first African American to become the Olympic individual all-around champion.

HALA AYALA
B.1973
A politician, Ayala is one of the first Hispanic women elected to the Virginia House of Delegates.

KEY FACTS

CAPITAL CITY
Richmond

TOTAL POPULATION OF STATE
8,631,393

AREA OF STATE (SQ MI)
42,775

POPULATION OF CAPITAL
226,610

SOLDIERS' RESTING PLACE

Nearly four million people visit Arlington National Cemetery to pay respect to America's fallen heroes. From military personnel to presidents like John F. Kennedy, the national cemetery hosts 400,000 graves and counting. Created in 1864, the area was first a regular estate owned by relatives of George Washington. When another cemetery for soldiers became full after the Civil War, the government purchased this land to honor its fallen servicemen. Arlington National Cemetery is a national treasure as well as a popular local destination. Today, America continues to honor its military and national heroes by burying them in this historic place.

ARLINGTON

BLACK-OWNED AND ORGANIC

Advocating for healthier food, the Black-owned organic farm, Sylvanaqua is a one-stop shop for food information and produce.

INDIGENOUS VIRGINIANS

Virginia is home to eight Indigenous American nations, including the Monacan, Nansemond, and Mattaponi, who primarily live in the Tidewater region.

HAMPTON PIRATES

Known for its pirate mascot, Hampton University is one of the state's historically Black Universities and home to 5,000 students.

FILIPINO CULTURE

In Henrico residents celebrate Filipino culture and cuisine with an annual festival featuring dance, art, and tasty dishes such as lumpia and adobo.

COIN-TOSS LOCKUP

In Richmond, it's technically against the law to flip a coin to determine who will pay for a cup of coffee!

HAMPTON ROADS

Beach lovers and military personnel live side by side in Hampton Roads, with its large army base and beautiful coastline.

RICHMOND

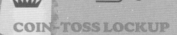

NORFOLK ✳ ✳ **VIRGINIA BEACH**

✳ **CHESAPEAKE**

HAM PATROL

Smithfield-area Virginians are serious about their ham! It's illegal to label ham as Smithfield unless it's genuine.

MILITARY TATTOOS

Norfolk residents celebrate music and dance with their annual International Tattoo, a musical performance by an actual military band.

CARIBBEAN FESTIVAL

Residents in Norfolk celebrate Caribbean and African folklore, music, and cuisine in their annual festival, CaribFest.

BOAT LOVERS

Known for its scenic waterfront properties, Virginia is home to hundreds of harbors and Norfolk hosts its annual Harborfest.

LATINO WASHINGTONIANS

Latinos have a long history in the state, beginning in 1775 when Spanish captain Juan Pérez led the ship *Santiago* from Mexico, to the coast of future Washington. Since 1970 they have been Washington's largest minority.

FERRY BOATS

People come from all over the Northwest to take a ride on the largest ferry system in the country and the second largest in the entire world!

GREAT GUITARISTS

Not only was the first electric guitar invented here, but the state also nurtured some great guitarists, including Kurt Cobain and Jimi Hendrix.

TURKFEST

Seattle has a sizable Turkish population who were originally drawn to the area by engineering jobs at Boeing and Microsoft. Over the years the community grew and now they celebrate their heritage with other locals through an annual festival called Turkfest!

INDIGENOUS WASHINGTONIANS

The state has over 29 federally recognized Indigenous tribal nations and 140,714 Indigenous citizens.

VIKING CITY

Poulsbo, near Seattle, is affectionately called Little Norway in honor of its Scandinavian founders. Each year it holds a Vikings Fest, which includes parades, dance, and music, to celebrate its heritage.

RAMBLING RAINFOREST

The state claims the only temperate rainforest in the continental U.S., the Hoh Rainforest.

SEATTLE

BELLEVUE

STARTUP MAGIC

Amazon, Microsoft, Costco, and Starbucks are part of a long list of hugely successful businesses that all began in this leading state for startups.

TACOMA

SEATTLE'S NIHONMACHI

Japanese communities have lived in Seattle since the Civil War, making up one of the largest J-towns or Nihonmachi on the West Coast!

ALIEN HUNTERS

Washingtonians tend to report the most UFO sightings in the world! They called in a sighting every two days in 2020.

OLYMPIA

SUNNY DAFFODILS!

Pierce County is a leading grower of the colorful daffodil, drawing huge crowds every year to an annual festival that features four parades!

UMOJA FEST

A decades-old festival celebrating the state's Black history and African heritage. Umoja—Swahili for "unity"— is the theme of the cultural extravaganza that showcases the music, dance, art, and diversity of the community!

WASHINGTON GARDENS

Washingtonians produce the most apples, pears, red raspberries, sweet cherries, and spearmint oil in the country. The fruitful soil is enriched by millennia of glacial water.

CHIEF KAMIAKIN (YAKAMA)
1800–1877
Leader of the Yakama, Palouse, and Klickitat peoples after whom the Yakama Indian Reservation is named.

VANCOUVER

BABY CARRIERS

The Yakama Nation is a confederacy of tribes whose people, like many other Indigenous groups, traditionally carried their babies on their backs in cradleboards.

WASHINGTON

People have lived in Washington for at least 10,000 years. They came from Asia across the ancient Bering Land Bridge during the last Ice Age. Thousands of years later, Indigenous Americans including the Yakama, Chinook, Nez Perce, and Puget Salish still lived on the land. In 1775, the Spanish arrived, and in the early 1800s the region was mapped as part of the famous Lewis and Clark Expedition. In 1889, Washington officially joined the Union as the 42nd state and the only one to be named after an American president.

This Pacific Northwestern state is nicknamed the "Evergreen State" because more than half of its land is covered in forests. It is famous for the Cascades, a mountain range that passes through Washington and which includes several volcanoes and vast areas covered by glaciers. The state is home to some of the nation's rainiest places, but this only adds to its lush natural beauty. Today, it's known for its plentiful hiking trails, whale watching opportunities, and its most delicious export: apples!

KEY FACTS

CAPITAL CITY
Olympia

TOTAL POPULATION OF STATE
7,705,281

AREA OF STATE (SQ MI)
71,298

POPULATION OF CAPITAL
55,605

DAM CONSTRUCTORS
Grand Coulee is one of the largest dams in the world! It took nearly 11,000 builders who worked more than 27 million hours to divert the river, excavate the foundation, and build this concrete giant.

SPOKANE

BERTHA KNIGHT LANDES
1868–1943
This mayor of Seattle was the first female mayor of any major American city.

JEFFREY DEAN MORGAN
B.1966
Actor best known for roles in *The Walking Dead* and *Supernatural*.

APOLO ANTON OHNO
B.1982
Eight-time Olympic medalist in speed skating. The most decorated American Olympian in the history of the Winter Olympics.

JEFF BEZOS
B.1964
Founder of Amazon and one of the first space tourists, who began his business in Washington.

FESTÁL
Festál is a series of free, annual festivals that highlight local diversity by giving various communities the stage to share their culture. Festál includes a Vietnamese Tết Festival, an Iranian Festival, BrasilFest, CroatiaFest, Hmong New Year Celebration, the Pagdiriwang Philippine Festival, Spirit of West Africa Festival, Festa Italiana, and a Mexican and Latin American festival called the Fiestas Patrias, among a host of others. The events draw in huge numbers who join to participate in a world's worth of experiences like dances, theater, musical ensembles, film, and colorful bazaars.

KEY FACTS

MUSICAL MARIMBAS
Marimba is a popular instrument and folk music style of El Salvador, with the largest group of Salvadoran Americans living in the D.C. area.

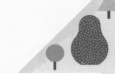

CHEVY CHASE

HISTORIC STRIVERS
The historic area of D.C. was home to notable African Americans like abolitionist Frederick Douglass and now hosts a diverse group of residents.

D.C. DRUMMERS
Every Sunday, hundreds of D.C. residents gather at Meridian Hill Park to participate in a decades-old drum circle tradition.

MULTITUDE OF FLAGS
Leaders from all over the world call one of the 170 embassies their temporary home while traveling in the United States.

ADAMS MORGAN

BLOOMINGDALE

SHAW

WASHINGTON

LITTLE ETHIOPIA
With flavorful aromas bursting from traditional East African restaurants, D.C. is home to the second largest population of Ethiopian Americans.

GROOVY GO-GOERS
Known as the official sound of D.C., go-go is a style of funk that attracts movers and shakers who love to beat their feet to the music.

RAINBOW PARADE
More than 200,000 residents visit Dupont Circle for its annual LGBTQ+ pride festival.

BLACK LIVES MATTER

FRIENDSHIP ARCHWAY
This gateway to D.C.'s Chinatown sees hundreds of visitors every week! It's one of the largest gateways outside of China.

MUMBO MUNCHERS
The ketchup-based sauce known as mumbo is a popular condiment for thousands of D.C. residents.

BLACK LIVES MATTER PLAZA
Not far from the White House residents can gather at the Black Lives Matter Plaza, a two-block long pedestrian area painted with 48-foot letters reminding us all to care about Black lives.

TASTE OF TEHRAN
With one of the highest populations of Iranian residents, popular Persian dishes offer flavor and culture in D.C.'s posh areas.

HISTORIC DYNASTY
D.C. is home to a small population of Uyghurs, an ethnic group from Central Asia. Most came to the U.S. seeking safety as refugees.

CHITA RIVERA
B.1933
The first Latina woman to be awarded the Presidential Medal of Freedom, Rivera is best known for her fancy footwork on Broadway.

SEASONAL DIPLOMAT
Senators from each state flock to Washington, D.C. for work during congressional sessions. These senators attract news and lobbyists from across the world.

LIBRARY LOVERS
The largest library in the world, the Library of Congress, is located on Capitol Hill.

FAST TRACK
With the second busiest Amtrak train station in the nation, D.C. residents can quickly visit cities like New York and Philadelphia and be back for dinner!

BILL NYE
B.1955
This zany science guy hosted one of the first science-centered TV shows for kids.

WASHINGTON D.C.

DAVE BAUTISTA
B.1969
A former wrestler, Bautista became an out-of-this world actor in a popular Marvel movie series.

CONNIE CHUNG
B.1946
As the first Asian American nightly news anchor, Chung made history for her popular interviews and style.

CORY BOOKER
B.1969
This dynamic politician is the first African American Senator of New Jersey. He has served as a mayor and run for President of the United States.

If you're looking for tons of history and culture, Washington, D.C., is the place to go. As the capital of the United States, visitors to this small city—it has an area of only 68 square miles—are never far from a historic document, monument, or museum. Founded in 1790, the region was named after America's first president, George Washington. "D.C." stands for "District of Columbia," the name given to this unique administrative region that is not part of any state.

The area has attracted diverse groups throughout the years, being one of the first hubs for freed slaves, and soon a destination for African Americans across the South. As the years went on, the city became home to communities from all over the world, including people from African, Asian, and Central and South American countries. This created a melting pot of cultures and ideas. During the civil rights movement, D.C. hosted one of the biggest protests in history, the March on Washington in 1963. The district continues to make history every day.

A MALL OF HISTORY
The National Mall is different to the malls in your hometown. This mall hosts over 24 million visitors a year! While there are no shopping stores, the area is home to historic museums like the Smithsonian, art galleries, memorials, and sculptures. It's a history buff's dream! The area is housed between the Lincoln Memorial and the U.S. Capitol. Bicyclists are often seen going for a relaxing ride, or sight-seeing in the area. This historic place has hosted protesters, festivals, and inaugurations.

SMITHSONIAN →

BEAU SMITH
B.1954
This comic book author is known for his work with DC Comics, and writing about characters like the Green Lantern.

KATHERINE JOHNSON
1918–2020
As one of the first African Americans at NASA, Johnson's calculations helped send astronauts to the Moon.

CHARLEY HARPER
1922–2007
A Modernist artist, Harper illustrated many natural landscapes in his unique style.

APPLE LOVERS
West Virginians love their apples! Since the late 1800s, locals have hosted carnivals to celebrate the apple harvest.

PICKIN' PAWPAWS
One of the state's best-kept secrets is the pawpaw fruit. Locals will tell you, eating just one is a treat!

COAL MINERS
Coal is one of the state's major resources, and nearly 14,000 residents work above and underground in coal mines.

WHEELING

ITALIAN CHRISTMAS
As an ode to local Italian culture, Fairmont celebrates the Christmas Eve tradition of feasting on various fish dishes and cannoli.

MORGANTOWN

BURR'S BASE
History buffs flock to Blennerhassett Island, a historic island with a replica of the estate where Aaron Burr allegedly plotted against the U.S.

PARKERSBURG

HISTORIC QUILTERS
Scottish and Irish settlers brought quilt-making to the state. West Virginia is known for a unique style of quilt recognizable by its contrasting borders.

GERMAN INFLUENCE
There is a strong German influence in the northwestern mountain area of the state, and almost 20% of West Virginians claim to have German ancestry.

STUFFED FARM
Residents of Point Pleasant boast a farming museum that offers a unique taxidermy collection, including the world's largest stuffed horse!

SOLAR-POWERED FUN
With a strong interest in environmental sustainability, locals enjoy a solar-powered music festival with the goal of promoting a cleaner environment.

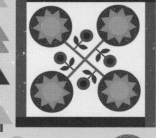

QUIET NEIGHBORS
In the National Radio Quiet Zone covering some of the Blue Ridge Mountains, people cannot use cell phones or wifi, so as not to interfere with military and scientific signals.

COAL MINERS REMEMBERED
Red Ash Island Cemetery is dedicated to members of the mining community who died in the 19th and early 20th centuries.

HUNTINGTON

CHARLESTON

APPALACHIAN CULTURE
Appalachian heritage is kept alive during an annual folk festival that celebrates the area's bluegrass music and square-dancing styles.

ROCK ART
At a site in Wyoming County, there are carvings, or petroglyphs, in the rock. Archaeologists believe they are the work of Indigenous artists.

SHUCK FOODIES
Shuck beans are one of the most popular dishes in Appalachian cuisine. They are green beans that have been strung on a thread and dried.

BRIDGE JUMPERS
One day a year, the state allows thrill-seekers to jump from the New River Bridge—it's nearly 900 feet tall!

KEY FACTS

CAPITAL CITY
Charleston

TOTAL POPULATION OF STATE
1,793,716

AREA OF STATE (SQ MI)
24,230

POPULATION OF CAPITAL
48,864

West Virginia

STEVE HARVEY
B.1957
This comedy king is an author and award-winning television host.

NICK SABAN
B.1951
Hailed as the greatest coach in college football history, Saban has won seven national titles as head coach.

With rolling hills and soaring mountains, West Virginia is a beautiful state with strong cultural traditions. Its parks and mountain views earned it the nickname "The Mountain State." This small region was also home to historic Indigenous groups such as the Cherokee, Haudenosaunee, and the Shawnee. West Virginia became a state in 1861, after separating from Virginia during the Civil War. It went on to become a key border state during the conflict.

Early settlers in the area included German, Irish, and Scottish people, who found fertile land perfect for potato farming. Many of the traditions brought by these settlers are still in practice today. Appalachian folk keep these traditions alive in cuisine, art, and song. The region is also home to many coal mines, as coal is one of its top resources. While a small state, West Virginia is a culturally rich area steeped in history.

GREEN BANK OBSERVERS
Green Bank is a special place in West Virginia. Here, the Green Bank Telescope is used in experiments ranging from chemistry and physics to radar receiving and astronomy. This massive telescope weighs 17 million pounds and searches for intelligent life in the universe! There is no other telescope in the world like it. Government scientists perform out-of-this-world research at the observatory. Visitors come to the area to see the massive telescope and learn more about the universe. Scientists using the Green Bank Telescope have discovered the simplest chemical building blocks of life at the center of our galaxy, the Milky Way.

Wisconsin

JOSEPH ZIMMERMANN
1912-2004
Inventor of the first answering machine, called the "Electronic Secretary" born in Kenosha.

MARK RUFFALO
B.1967
Actor born in Kenosha, famous for many roles such as Marvel's Hulk.

HANK "HAMMERIN'" AARON
1934-2021
An icon in the Badger State for being a life-long Wisconsin baseball player, an All-Star 21 times, and setting a home run record.

GINSENG FARMERS
Marathon County produces nearly all of the ginseng grown in the U.S. and about 10% of the world's supply. Locals host an annual festival to celebrate this humble root.

RESILIENT REPUBLICANS
The Republican Party was founded in Ripon at a meeting at the Little White Schoolhouse. Part of the original reason it came into existence was to combat slavery.

PUNK ROCKERS!
Wisconsinites have a rich history of punk rocking. Milwaukee and Green Bay have set the scene for the colorful genre since the 1980s—new bands are still rocking today!

ICE CREAM LOVERS
The first ever ice cream sundae was served in Two Rivers in 1881. The sweet treats are a major draw to the original shop, the Washington House, for ice cream lovers.

CHAINSAW ARTISTS
The U.S. Open Chainsaw Sculpture Championship hosts the world's best chainsaw carvers, who create intricately detailed works of art out of wooden logs.

CRANBERRY GROWERS
Although Warrens only has 400 residents, it draws 100,000 visitors each September for the world's largest cranberry festival. Wisconsin produces 60% of American cranberries.

BIRTHPLACE OF THE REPUBLICAN PARTY
RIPON, WIS.

GREEN BAY

SUBMARINE BUILDERS
The Wisconsin Maritime Museum honors Manitowoc's history of sub-builders with their own festival!

SUMMER SPLASH!
Wisconsin Dells has the largest concentration of water parks in the world! Thrill seekers slide down more than 200 water slides and splash around in 16 million gallons of water combined.

WISCONSIN CHEESE

CHEESE HEADS!
Known as "America's Dairyland," Wisconsin maintains its Dutch heritage as the number one producer of cheese in the U.S. It is the only state where you can study to become a Master Cheesemaker!

MADISON

MILWAUKEE

RACINE

KENOSHA

KEY FACTS

CAPITAL CITY
Madison

TOTAL POPULATION OF STATE
5,893,718

AREA OF STATE (SQ MI)
65,496

POPULATION OF CAPITAL
269,840

MUSTARD MAKERS
National Mustard Day in Middleton is where all the mustard magic happens! Mustard games, live music and entertainment, and even "mustard custard" bring out the whole town!

INDIGENOUS LEGACY
Effigy mounds—raised piles of earth built in the shape of animals, symbols, or other figures—were built by Indigenous communities throughout Wisconsin. They're just the tip of an iceberg of rich and vibrant history.

FONDUE FEST

Wisconsin's award-winning history of cheesemaking inspires the Fondue Fest held in Fond du Lac every year. The 8-foot-wide fondue pot—which holds over 4,000 pounds of melty cheese—is just one of the star attractions! Fondue Fest also features live music, fondue tastings, a rubber-duck race, tons of vendors, a car show, and a fondue-eating contest!

MIDWEST SURFING

Freshwater surfers know Sheboygan as the "Malibu of the Midwest." But the peak surf season takes place in the winter, between September and March... brrr!

VEL PHILLIPS
1923–2018

The first African American to become a judge in Wisconsin. In 1978, Phillips was elected secretary of state for Wisconsin, making her the first African American woman elected to a statewide office in the nation!

CHIEF OSHKOSH
1795–1858

Chief of the Menominee Indigenous nation, who played a key role in treaty negotiations to protect their lands in Wisconsin.

BLACK HISTORY

America's Black Holocaust Museum in Milwaukee is a memorial museum dedicated to the history of Black oppression and struggle in America.

POLONIA

More than 200,000 Milwaukeeans trace their roots to Poland, making Milwaukee one of the capitals of Polish America! The Basilica of St. Josaphat was founded in 1888 by Polish immigrants, and it remains a source of enormous pride for the Polish American community.

THE CASABLANCA HOTEL

In Milwaukee's Harambee neighborhood, this home-turned-hotel housed touring Black jazz artists who weren't allowed to stay at the city's other hotels. Guests included Louis Armstrong, Duke Ellington, Sarah Vaughan, and Billie Holiday.

Mammoth hunters lived in Wisconsin nearly 14,500 years ago. Indigenous communities formed thousands of years after the hunters arrived, including the Dakota Sioux, Winnebago, Menominee, Ojibwe, Potawatomi, Fox, and Sauk. Eleven of these tribal nations still live in Wisconsin today. The French and British arrived in the 1700s, and the British fur traders eventually gained control. In 1848, Wisconsin became the 30th American state.

Wisconsin is a Midwestern state with more than 15,000 lakes carved by prehistoric glaciers. It is covered with woodlands, flatlands, and flat-top hills called buttes and mesas. The Badger State is known for its world-class supply of cheese and ginseng, and its sizable German and Polish populations. Among its lesser-known claims to fame are its status as the "toilet-paper capital of the world" for producing the first splinter-free paper, and as the site of the first kindergarten class in the U.S.!

CAPITAL CITY
Cheyenne

TOTAL POPULATION OF STATE
576,851

AREA OF STATE (SQ MI)
97,813

POPULATION OF CAPITAL
65,132

ALONZO STEPP
1874–1941
One of the first African American homesteaders, who built a prosperous ranch where the Fontenelle Reservoir is now.

WORLD-CLASS ICE CLIMBING
South Fork Canyon, near Cody, boasts some of the best frozen waterfalls in North America! A festival there hosts ice-climbers from around the world.

YELLOWSTONE DIVERSITY
Yellowstone attracts all types of people, including trail riders, conservationists, researchers, and even wolf trackers! People come from across the country and around the world to work, explore, and enjoy the wilderness!

POWWOW PRIDE
Dancers and drummers from around the nation compete at the Plains Indian Museum Powwow, an annual cultural celebration near Cody.

ELK COUNTRY
The National Elk Refuge is a sanctuary for one of the largest elk herds on Earth! Locals help feed nearly 7,000 elk so they can survive long winters, and visitors can take sleigh rides to explore the area.

ISLAND HOPPERS
Wyoming may be landlocked, but it's home to dozens of islands in lakes! In the winter, tours are done on skis.

WORLDLY MOUNTAINEERS
Drawing climbers from all over the globe, Lander hosts a three-day International Climbers' Festival on the upper plains of the Rockies.

CLARENCE CLAYTON DANKS
1879–1970
Rodeo royalty who won the Cheyenne Frontier Days rodeo three times, and may have inspired one of Wyoming's state symbols, the "Bucking Horse and Rider."

MOUNTAIN MEN
Recreating the Indigenous American and Rocky Mountain fur trade history of the area, the Green River Rendezvous festival includes historic presentations and an authentic traders' row.

ROCK SPRINGS

GOLD RUSHERS
In celebration of life in a western gold camp, South Pass City State Historic Site hosts Gold Rush Days. These showcase a vintage baseball tournament, gold panning, live music in saloons, and reenactments.

THE CHEYENNE FRONTIER DAYS RODEO
Wyoming's official state sport is rodeo. The Cheyenne Frontier Days rodeo is one of the largest of them all! It includes ten days of competitions, concerts featuring national country music acts, a carnival, a horse-filled Grand Parade, an Indigenous American village complete with traditional dancers, and an art show.

DUDE RANCHERS
Eatons' Ranch was the first ranch opened by the state as a tourist attraction. Also known as a "dude ranch," it's a perfect stop for visitors to learn about ranching life.

INDIGENOUS ASTRONOMERS
In Bighorn, there is a circle of stones called a medicine wheel, which Plains tribes between 800 and 300 years ago may have used to predict the position of the Sun.

GILLETTE

THE DINOSAUR STATE
Wyoming has been an important destination for fossil hunters for two centuries. Dinosaur bones are so plentiful that a local elementary school discovered an entire skull and other bones on a field trip!

CASPER

COAL MINERS
Wyoming is home to two of the world's largest coal mines. Wyomingites produce nearly half of America's coal.

BLACK HOMESTEADERS
After the Civil War, African Americans communities founded settlements like Empire as places to live away from racist discrimination.

UP, UP IN THE AIR!
The Riverton Rendezvous Hot Air Balloon Rally celebrates the town's founding in 1906 with balloon launches every year. Hot air balloon pilots from all over the country participate, with their balloons lighting up the sky in dazzling colors.

LEADING WOMEN
Wyomingites have elected women to the House of Representatives in nearly 80% of elections since 1989. That's the highest percentage in the country!

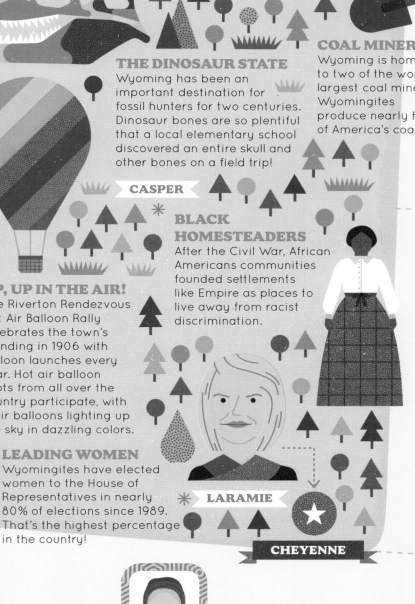

LARAMIE

CHEYENNE

MARGARET THOMAS "MARDY" MURIE
1902–2003
Known as the "Grandmother of the Conservation Movement," Murie devoted her life to preserving the wilderness.

ZARIF KHAN
1887–1964
Afghan immigrant and one of the first Muslims in Wyoming. Khan became a local legend as "Hot Tamale Louie," selling the Mexican delicacies from his cart-turned-restaurant in Sheridan.

CHIEF WASHAKIE
C.1804/1810–1900
A Shoshone leader who was famous for his successful, peaceful dealings with the U.S. government, which ensured his people had their own territory.

Wyoming was inhabited at least 12,000 years ago. Thousands of years later Indigenous Americans including the Arapaho, Cheyenne, Crow, Shoshone, and Ute lived on the land. Throughout the 18th and 19th centuries, various countries laid claim to the region, including Spain, France, Great Britain, and Mexico. In 1848, Wyoming was claimed as a U.S. territory, but Indigenous Americans continued to fight for their rights to live on the land. It wasn't until 1890 that it became the 44th state.

Named after a Munsee Delaware word for "at the big river flat," Wyoming is split between the Great Plains and the Rocky Mountains. It has the lowest population in the country, and was the first in the nation to grant women the right to vote and become politicians. The Equality State is famous for its epic scenery. It is filled with dazzling national parks and a diverse variety of wildlife, including the famous American bison. Peppered with pioneer and cowboy towns, it's been the inspiration behind countless Western novels, and has treasure troves of fossils to keep dinosaur enthusiasts digging.

WYOMING

CAPITAL CITY
Charlotte
Amalie

TOTAL POPULATION OF TERRITORY
106,290

AREA OF TERRITORY (SQ MI)
733

POPULATION OF CAPITAL
18,481

CRICKET, ANYONE?
A popular sport on the islands, cricket players compete internationally as part of the West Indies.

PUERTO RICAN INFLUENCE
Puerto Ricans migrated to the area in the mid-1900s to work in the sugar industry. They represent over 10% of the population.

JEWISH COMMUNITIES
St. Thomas is home to one of the oldest Jewish communities in the Western Hemisphere, the Sephardi Jewish people.

AUDRE LORDE
1934–1992
An acclaimed essayist and poet, Lorde is hailed as one of the most influential African American feminist writers in history.

CHARLOTTE AMALIE

CRUZ BAY

U.S. VIRGIN ISLANDS

CALLIX CRABBE
B.1983
This famous professional baseball star was a second baseman for the San Diego Padres.

KELSEY GRAMMER
B.1955
Award-winning actor, producer, and director best known for roles in *Cheers*, *Frasier*, and *The Simpsons*.

NEIGHBORLY LOVE
Residents celebrate Virgin Islands–Puerto Rico Friendship Day to honor Puerto Ricans who live or have made contributions to the area.

AWESOME OKRA
Known as a staple of Caribbean cuisine like fungi and callaloo, okra is a popular food item across the islands and among African-influenced areas.

SAINT CROIX

HELLO
HAIL UP

BULL AND BREAD CELEBRATION
This celebration invites residents to commemorate David Hamilton Jackson, a leader in civil and workers' rights movements.

COOL CRUCIAN
This dialect is a form of creole English spoken by people on the island of St. Croix.

The U.S. Virgin Islands are a group of Caribbean islands that were organized as a territory of the U.S in 1917. The main islands are St. Croix, St. John, and St. Thomas, but there are dozens of smaller islands that also make up the territory. Known for their beautiful weather, flawless ocean views, and delectable cuisine, these islands attract over two million visitors each year. While tourism is their biggest industry, other enterprises include agriculture and manufacturing. The island boasts a strong African-influenced culture, and there is also a growing Hispanic population that adds to the dynamic island lifestyle.

puerto rico

REGGAETON RHYTHM
Reggaeton blends hip-hop with Caribbean musical styles. Legendary San Juan club The Noise helped birth this influential genre, in the 1990s.

CATHOLIC COMMUNITY
Over 50% of Puerto Ricans are Catholic, and some of the oldest Catholic churches in the Americas are in San Juan.

AFRICAN INSPIRATION
Bomba is a dance and musical style brought to Puerto Rico by enslaved Africans. Bomba dances often spill out onto the streets of San Juan!

SAN JUAN
BAYAMON
CAROLINA
CAGUAS
PONCE

SALSA DANCERS
The most popular dance in Puerto Rico, these dancers offer free classes and salsa night parties across the island.

TAÍNO CULTURE
Thousands of Puerto Ricans bake cassava bread, a Taíno tradition dating back to the 15th century.

PINEAPPLE PICKERS
A staple of Taíno culture, pineapple farmers maintain over 365 acres of fresh juicy pineapples.

FLAVORFUL FOODIES
Puertor Ricans love hearty meals. Arroz con gandules is a tasty rice-based meal that is considered the island's national dish.

RICKY MARTIN
B.1971
With saucy dance moves, this artist is known as the most influential Latino performer of his time.

LIN-MANUEL MIRANDA
B.1980
History has its eyes on this Broadway mega star, who broke records as a Pulitzer Prize-winning writer, composer, and actor.

RITA MORENO
B.1931
This iconic dancer, actress, and singer is one of few EGOTs: someone who has won an Emmy, Grammy, Oscar, and Tony award.

Puerto Rico is a beautiful island with a distinct culture and history. For hundreds of years it was inhabited by the indigenous Taíno people, until Spanish settlers colonized the area. In 1898, the U.S. raised the flag on the island after defeating the Spanish in the Spanish–American War. As Americans, Puerto Ricans are an integral part of the nation's diverse history, contributing hugely to the arts, music, and cuisine of the nation. The territory is the only part of America where Spanish is the primary language. With picturesque beach views and lush scenery, the Spanish Caribbean culture of the island is alive and well.

KEY FACTS

CAPITAL CITY
San Juan

TOTAL POPULATION OF TERRITORY
3,285,874

AREA OF TERRITORY (SQ MI)
5,325

POPULATION OF CAPITAL
322,854

NORTHERN MARIANA ISLANDS

AGRIHAN

PAGAN

ALAMAGAN

DIVERS
The islands are filled with breathtaking dive sites. Saipan alone boasts some of the best in the world, where divers can explore unique coral reefs, caves, caverns, and even World War II shipwrecks!

ISLAND DIVERSITY
Nearly 50% of islanders are of Asian heritage, including Filipino, Korean, Chinese, Bangladeshi, Japanese, and Indonesian. The other major community is Pacific Islanders, such as the CHamoru, Palauan, and Carolinian. The mix of people creates a unique blend of island cuisine like the CHamoru-influenced kelaguen, Filipino-inspired pancit and Spanish empanadas.

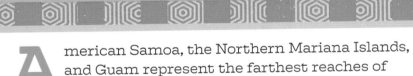

MAHI MAHI FISHING DERBY
Saipan Fishermen's Association hosts an annual fishing competition to which more than 100 fishers come from throughout Guam and the Northern Mariana Islands to compete.

MARIANAS WINDS KITE FESTIVAL & CULTURAL FOOD FAIR
In celebration of the diverse community and breezy island weather, the islands host a kite festival. Alongside cuisine from around the world, they award kite-flyers titles like Most Whimsical, Longest Tail, and Most Beautiful.

MATÅ'PANG
D.1680
A CHamoru maga'låhi, or chief, on the island of Guahan, known for resisting the Spanish invasion during the Spanish–Chamorro Wars. He is iconic among today's activists for CHamoru self-determination.

JON SAKOVICH
B.1970
Award-winning swimmer from Saipan who has represented Guam and the U.S. at the Olympics.

American Samoa, the Northern Mariana Islands, and Guam represent the farthest reaches of the U.S. But despite their humble size and remote locations, these three island groups have had a considerable influence on American and world culture.

The first people to live in Samoa, the Lapita, came from Indonesia, Fiji, and Vanuatu over 3,000 years ago. Their culture is believed to be the oldest in Polynesia, the Pacific region to which Samoa belongs. Samoa gained independence from New Zealand in 1962. Its neighbor to the southeast, American Samoa, became a U.S. territory in 1925. It is famous for delicious tuna, incredible marine life, and footballers!

The Northern Mariana Islands and Guam have been home to the CHamoru people of Micronesia for over 3,500 years. The U.S. took control of the Northern Mariana Islands from Germany after World War II. Today, they are known for their breathtaking natural sights as well as a calendar full of fairs and celebrations.

Guam has been a U.S. territory since 1898. This "Island of Warriors" sees the first sunrise on American soil, and its island culture comes to life in festivals, art, and cuisine.

SAIPAN

SAN JOSE

SINAPALU

KEY FACTS

CAPITAL CITY
Saipan

TOTAL POPULATION OF COMMONWEALTH
57,557

AREA OF COMMONWEALTH (SQ MI)
1,976

POPULATION OF CAPITAL
48,220

GENDER DIVERSITY

In Samoa, fa'afafine and fa'afatama are people who are neither male nor female. They hold unique, traditional roles in society, including as carers and educators.

TATTOOING

Samoan tatau art is more than 2,000 years old! It is one of the oldest tattoo traditions and is a Polynesian rite of passage. The custom is showcased and celebrated at annual events like Tisa's Tattoo Festival in Tutuila.

INDIGENOUS SAMOANS

Samoans are a Polynesian people closely related to the indigenous peoples of New Zealand, French Polynesia, Hawaii, and Tonga. Nine out of ten people in American Samoa identify as Samoan, but there are communities of Tongan and Filipino origin well.

FOOTBALL ISLAND

The islands earned this nickname for raising more American football players than anywhere else in the world! Young American Samoan men are 56 times more likely to play in the NFL than other young males in America.

DWAYNE "THE ROCK" JOHNSON
B.1972

This former professional wrestler is now one of the world's highest-grossing actors, and has always honored his Samoan heritage in the ring and on screen.

TROY POLAMALU
B.1981

Four-time All-Pro, two-time Super Bowl Champion, Hall of Fame football player. While in the NFL, he refused to cut his hair and wore it down during games in recognition of his Samoan heritage.

LALOMOANA

PAGO PAGO

TĀFUNA

TA'Ū

KEY FACTS

CAPITAL CITY
Pago Pago

TOTAL POPULATION OF TERRITORY
55,197

AREA OF TERRITORY (SQ MI)
581

POPULATION OF CAPITAL
3,656

GUAM

KEY FACTS

CAPITAL CITY
Hagåtña

TOTAL POPULATION OF TERRITORY
168,783

AREA OF TERRITORY (SQ MI)
571

POPULATION OF CAPITAL
1,051

YIGO

DEDEDO

HAGÅTÑA

RAY ROBSON
B.1994

At nine years old, Robson defeated a National Master in chess and is one of the youngest players in history to become a chess Grandmaster.

DONOVAN PATTON
B.1978

Actor best known for his role as Joe, the second host of the children's show *Blue's Clues*.

FILIPINO HERITAGE

Together with other Pacific Islanders, Guam's Filipino and CHamoru communities share cultural, linguistic, and colonial histories. Today, Filipinos make up the second largest ethnic community in Guam.

RED-HOT CHILIES

Donne Festival highlights a central spice in local CHamoru cuisine and Guam's signature dipping sauce, finadene. Local farmers and horticulturalists display rows of produce and plants, including their famous pepper plants.

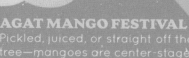

AGAT MANGO FESTIVAL

Pickled, juiced, or straight off the tree—mangoes are center-stage at this three-day fair! Local families grow different varieties of mango in their yards and ranches. Each family presents a basket of their harvest, displaying a variety of the fruit found on the island.

GUAM MICRONESIA ISLAND FAIR

The fair is the largest annual celebration of cultural diversity in Micronesia and the Western Pacific. People from nations like Palau, Yap, Pohnpei, Kosrae, and the Marshall Islands come together to celebrate art, performance, and traditions unique to their islands.

index

Brimming with creative inspiration, how-to projects, and useful information to enrich your everyday life, quarto.com is a favorite destination for those pursuing their interests and passions.

First published in 2022 by Wide Eyed Editions, an imprint of The Quarto Group.
100 Cummings Center, Suite 265D, Beverly, MA 01915, USA.
T +1 978-282-9590 F +1 078-283-2742 www.Quarto.com

ISBN 978-0-7112-6906-4

The illustrations were created digitally
Set in Quicksand, Hatch, and Cream

Published by Georgia Amson-Bradshaw
Designed by Kevin Knight and Sasha Moxon
Edited by Claire Grace
Editorial Assistant: Rachel Robinson
Production by Dawn Cameron

Manufactured in Guangdong, China CC072022

9 8 7 6 5 4 3 2 1

STATE FLAGS

OF THE UNITED STATES

ALABAMA

ALASKA

ARIZONA

ARKANSAS

CALIFORNIA

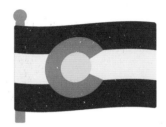
COLORADO

CONNECTICUT

DELAWARE

FLORIDA

GEORGIA

HAWAII

IDAHO

ILLINOIS

INDIANA

IOWA

KANSAS

KENTUCKY

LOUISIANA

MAINE

MARYLAND

MASSACHUSETTS

MICHIGAN

MINNESOTA

MISSISSIPPI

MISSOURI

MONTANA